✔ KU-174-944

PENGUI
PL34

THE RULES OF THE GAME
THE LIFE I GAVE YOU
LAZARUS

LUIGI PIRANDELLO

LUIGI PIRANDELLO

The Rules of the Game
The Life I Gave You
Lazarus

INTRODUCED AND EDITED BY
E. MARTIN BROWNE

PENGUIN BOOKS

Penguin Books Ltd, Harmondsworth, Middlesex
AUSTRALIA: Penguin Books Pty Ltd, 762 Whitehorse Road,
Mitcham, Victoria

—

Il gioco delle parti first published 1919
This translation first published 1959 in Penguin Books
Copyright © the heirs of Luigi Pirandello and
Robert Rietty, 1959

La vita che ti diedi first published 1924
This translation first published 1959 in Penguin Books
Copyright © the heirs of Luigi Pirandello and
Frederick May, 1959

Lazzaro first published 1929
This translation first published 1959 in Penguin Books
Copyright © the heirs of Luigi Pirandello and
Frederick May, 1959

Made and printed in Great Britain
by Unwin Brothers Limited
Woking and London

CONTENTS

INTRODUCTION

TWENTY years after his death, the English theatre is still almost totally neglecting Luigi Pirandello. Yet he is one of the greatest masters of the contemporary drama; and the word 'contemporary' still applies to him as it does to few of those who lived in his time. I hope that the publication in this series of two volumes of his plays may widen the interest in him and perhaps lead to more of his plays being produced in English.

Pirandello was born in 1867, and grew up with the sentimentality of later nineteenth-century literature as his staple food. He was the foremost amongst those in Italy, the Futurists as they called themselves, who reacted violently against it. While he was developing his talent by writing novels and short stories, several lesser dramatists were preparing the way for him in the Italian theatre. The 'Teatro del Grottesco' sought to break away from the well-made play by bringing on to the stage situations of a bizarre or fantastic kind, and treating them with an exaggerated humour. The most famous and successful of these plays was Luigi Chiarelli's *The Mask and the Face*, a brilliantly funny caricature of the romantic drama which allows a serious idea to be developed within itself. Pirandello uses the same approach for purposes more profound, for to him the drama must be the expression of the intellect: 'One of the novelties that I have given to drama', he says, 'consists in converting the intellect into passion.' But let it not be supposed that Pirandello relies on the intellectual content of his plays to replace the craftsmanship of the playwright. On the contrary, most of them are extremely well constructed and hold our interest quite apart from what they have to say.

Pirandello was a Sicilian, born in Girgenti where the Greek temples stand ruined amidst some of the island's most picturesque scenery. His father was a rich proprietor of sulphur mines, a strong, overbearing man. When Luigi was a young man, floods destroyed the mines, and the family was reduced to poverty. For Luigi this was the cause of a far worse disaster. He had been married by his father to a woman who was driven by their financial troubles into an hysterical form of insanity. Unreasoningly jealous, she made his life a hell; but he endured it until in 1919 she entered a nursing home. This

7

is the background against which his imagination worked, and accounts for the intensification of his pessimism.

The problem of the nature of personality, which has dominated philosophical thinking in this century, is acute for Pirandello, and perhaps more so because he must have lived for so many years a double life, as himself and as the twisted version of himself in his wife's mind. He may have wondered which was the real self: certainly his characters wrestle with such doubts. His plays stimulate reflection upon the mystery of life, which is in perpetual flux, the nature of which we no sooner think we have grasped than it slips away from us, the truth of which we really prefer to hide from ourselves by illusions since we know we can never pin it down.

Some of Pirandello's drama appears cold, because it is concerned with thought rather than emotion; but there is no lack of emotion in his characters. *The Rules of the Game* (*Il gioco delle parti*, 1919) has for its chief character Leone Gala, who provokes his feckless wife into involving him in a duel, by his apparent indifference to her affair with Guido, and then by refusing with ironic humour to fight for her he condemns her lover to be killed in his place. But at the final climax of the play Leone denounces his hated rival with all the passionate fury of a hero of the old melodrama.

The Life I Gave You (*La vita che ti diedi*, 1924) is a study of resurrection in another sense: the life which is transferred from one person to another through the strength of love. The characters are deeply understood, and Donna Anna, the mother who in giving up her grandchild-to-be loses her son a second time, is a truly tragic figure.

This and the last play concern life and death, and complement each other in their exposition of Pirandello's philosophy. *Lazarus* (*Lazzaro*, 1929) is notable as the most complete expression of his religious views. The young man in his cassock, whose faith has been restored to him through his father's resurrection, cries: 'Your soul *is* God, father. And you call it yours. It is God, don't you see? … If our soul is God within us, what else would you call His science and a miracle achieved by means of it, if not one of His miracles, wrought when He would have it accomplished?'

This is a play of great strength and sincerity; the attempt of a man who was brought up in a Catholic country full of modern philosophy to reconcile the two ways of approach to the meaning of life.

THE RULES OF THE GAME

Il gioco delle parti

TRANSLATED BY ROBERT RIETTY

For permission to perform this play and for the right to use this translation apply to the International Copyright Bureau, 26 Charing Cross Road, London WC2.

This play was first presented in England in this translation at the Arts Theatre, London, 13 January 1955, with the following cast:

LEONE	*Donald Pleasance*
SILIA	*Melissa Stribling*
GUIDO	*Robert Cartland*
SPIGA	*Dudley Jones*
BARELLI	*Peter Whitbread*
PHILIP	*Gilbert Davis*
MIGLIORITI	*Eric Hillyard*
CLARA	*Silia Sherry*
1ST DRUNK	*Timothy Bateson*
2ND DRUNK	*Stewart Weller*
1ST TENANT	*Frank Royd*
2ND TENANT	*Lucille Lee*
3RD TENANT	*Joan Harrison*

Produced by John Fernald

CHARACTERS

LEONE GALA

SILIA GALA, Leone's Wife

GUIDO VENANZI, Silia's Lover

DOCTOR SPIGA

BARELLI

PHILIP (nicknamed SOCRATES), Leone's Servant

MARQUIS MIGLIORITI

CLARA, Silia's Maid

THREE DRUNK YOUNG 'MEN-ABOUT-TOWN'

SEVERAL TENANTS of floors above and below Silia's flat

SCENE: Any town in Italy

TIME: The present

ACT ONE

The smartly furnished drawing-room of Silia Gala's flat.

At the back, a large double sliding door, painted white, with red glass panes in the upper panels, divides this room from the dining-room.

The front door and a window are on the Left.

In the Right-hand wall there is a fireplace, and on the mantel-piece an ormolu clock. Near the fireplace, another door leads to a third room.

When the curtain rises, both sections of the glass door are slid right back into the wall.

The time is about 10.15 p.m.

[GUIDO VENANZI, in evening dress, is standing by the dining-room table, on which a number of liqueur bottles can be seen in a silver stand.

SILIA GALA, in a light dressing-gown, is in the drawing-room, huddled up day-dreaming in an armchair.]

GUIDO: Chartreuse?

[He waits for an answer. SILIA ignores him.]

Anisette?

[Same result.]

Cognac? Well? Shall I choose?

[He pours out a glass of anisette, and takes it to SILIA.]

Here, try this.

[SILIA still takes no notice, and remains motionless for a few seconds. Then, shuddering with annoyance at finding him near her with the glass in his hand, she utters an exclamation of irritation. GUIDO, annoyed, drinks the glass in one gulp.]

GUIDO [bowing]: Thanks for the trouble! I didn't really want it.

[SILIA *resumes her original attitude.* GUIDO *puts down the glass, sits down, and turns to look at her.*]

You might at least tell me what's the matter with you.

SILIA: If you imagine I'm here . . .

GUIDO: Oh, so you're not here? You're somewhere else, I suppose?

SILIA [*furiously*]: Yes, I am somewhere else! Miles away!

GUIDO [*quietly, after a pause, as though to himself*]: Then I'm alone, eh? In that case, I may as well see if there's anything worth stealing here.

[*He gets up and pretends to search about the room.*]

Let me see . . . a few paintings. N – no, too modern! Silver . . . hardly worth troubling about!

[*He approaches* SILIA *as though he does not see her. When quite close to her he stops with an expression of mock surprise.*]

Hullo! What's this? Your body left behind in the chair? I shall certainly take that! [*He tries to embrace her.*]

SILIA [*jumping to her feet and pushing him away*]: Stop it! I tell you I won't have it!

GUIDO: Oh, pity! You're back again already! Your husband is right when he says our only real trips abroad are the ones we make in our imagination.

SILIA: You know, that's the fourth or fifth time you've mentioned *him* tonight.

GUIDO: It seems to be the only way of getting you to talk to me.

SILIA: No, Guido, it only makes you more of a bore.

GUIDO: Thanks!

SILIA [*after a long pause, with a sigh, distantly*]: I saw it all so clearly!

GUIDO: What did you see?

SILIA: I must have read about it, I suppose. But everything was so clear and vivid. A woman, sitting there, smiling to herself as she worked.

14

GUIDO: What was she doing?

SILIA: I don't know – I couldn't see her hands. But it was something women do while their men are away fishing. I think it's in Iceland. Yes, that's where it is.

GUIDO: You were dreaming you were in . . . Iceland?

SILIA: Yes, I was day-dreaming. But that's the way I always travel. [*Pause.*] It's got to stop! It's got to stop! [*Aggressively.*] This can't go on any longer.

GUIDO: You're referring to me, I suppose?

SILIA: I'm referring to myself.

GUIDO: But don't you see that anything that concerns you concerns me too?

SILIA [*annoyed*]: Oh, God! You always see everything on such a tiny scale. You're shut up in a smug little cut-and-dried world of your own, where nothing is allowed to exist that doesn't concern you personally. I bet geography still means nothing more to you than a textbook, and a map on a schoolroom wall!

GUIDO [*puzzled*]: Geography?

SILIA: Yes. Didn't your teacher set you lists of names to be learnt by heart for homework?

GUIDO: Lord, yes! What a bore!

SILIA: But rivers, mountains, countries, islands, continents – they really *do* exist, you know.

GUIDO [*sarcastically*]: Really? Thanks for telling me!

SILIA: And there are people living there – and all the time we're cooped up in this room.

GUIDO [*as though light had suddenly dawned on him*]: Ah, I see. You're hinting that I ought to take you abroad.

SILIA: There you go again! I make a perfectly general statement, and you immediately think it must have some bearing on our situation. I'm not hinting at anything. I'm merely trying to 'broaden your outlook'; to make you think a little about all the different lives other people live. I can't bear this life any longer. I'm stifled!

GUIDO: But what sort of life *do* you want?

SILIA: I don't know. Any life that's different from this! God, if I could only see the faintest glimmer of hope for the future! I tell you I'd be perfectly happy just basking in that ray of hope – without running to flatten my nose against the window-pane to see what there is in store for me outside.

GUIDO: You're talking as if you were in a prison!

SILIA: I am in prison!

GUIDO: Oh? Who's keeping you there?

SILIA: You, and everyone else! Even my own body, because I can never forget that it's a woman's. How can I, when you men are always staring at my figure? I never think about my body, until I catch men's eyes ogling. Often I burst out laughing. 'Well,' I say to myself, 'there's no getting away from it – I *am* a woman!'

GUIDO: I don't think you've any reason to complain about that.

SILIA: Because I'm attractive? [*Pause.*] But can't you see that all . . . *this* is mainly due to my being continually reminded I'm a woman, and forced to be one when I don't want to be?

GUIDO [*slowly, detached*]: Tonight, for example.

SILIA: Being a woman has never given *me* any pleasure.

GUIDO: Not even the pleasure of making a man miserable?

SILIA: Yes, *that* perhaps. Often.

GUIDO [*as before*]: Tonight, for example.

[*Pause.* SILIA *sits absorbed.*]

SILIA [*fretfully*]: But one's own life! . . . the life we don't share with anybody – not even ourselves . . .

GUIDO: What *are* you talking about?

SILIA: Haven't you ever stood gazing at your reflection in a mirror, without thinking about yourself? Suddenly you feel that your face belongs to someone else, a stranger, and you study it intently. Then you see a stray lock of hair, or something – automatically you push it back into place, and immediately the spell is broken, everything is spoilt.

GUIDO: Yes – well?

SILIA: Other people's eyes are like a mirror – so are our own, when we are using them to look at ourselves to find out the way we ought to live; the way we are bound to live, in fact. Oh, I can't explain!

[*A pause.*]

GUIDO [*approaching*]: Shall I tell you frankly why you're getting so worked up?

SILIA [*promptly*]: Because you're here – standing in front of me!

GUIDO [*taking it to heart*]: Oh! In that case would you like me to go?

SILIA: Yes, you had better.

GUIDO: But why, Silia?

[SILIA *shrugs her shoulders.*]

Why do you treat me so badly?

SILIA: I'm not treating you badly. I don't want people to see you here too often, that's all.

GUIDO: Too often! Why, I hardly ever come here. It must be more than a week since I was here last. Obviously time passes too quickly for you.

SILIA: Quickly? Every day seems an eternity!

GUIDO [*close*]: Then why do you pretend that I count for nothing in your life? Silia . . . [*He tries to embrace her.*]

SILIA [*irritated*]: Oh, for heaven's sake, Guido!

GUIDO: I've waited for you day after day. You hardly let me see you any more . . .

SILIA: But don't you see the state I'm in?

GUIDO: That's simply because you don't know what you want. You go and invoke some vague hope or other that will open a chink for you into the future.

SILIA: According to you, I suppose I ought to go forward to meet the future with a ruler in my hand to measure all my desires. 'So much I may allow myself to want, and no more.' It's like doling out sweets to a child!

GUIDO: I expect you think I'm being pedantic!

SILIA: Yes, I do. All this you're saying bores me stiff!

GUIDO: Thanks!

SILIA: You want to make me believe that I have had everything I could wish for, and that I'm getting 'worked up'
like this now – as you put it – because I'm snatching at something out of reach – at the impossible. Isn't that it? [*Mimick-
ing him.*] 'It's not reasonable!' Oh, I know that! But what
would you have me do? I *do* want the impossible!

GUIDO: What, for instance?

SILIA: Can you tell me what I've had out of life to make me
happy?

GUIDO: Happiness is all a question of degree. One person is
satisfied with little; another has everything, and is never
satisfied.

SILIA: Do you imagine I have everything?

GUIDO: No, but you're never content with things as they are.
What on earth *are* you hankering after?

SILIA [*as though to herself*]: I want to be rich . . . my own mistress . . . free! [*Suddenly flaring up.*] Haven't you understood
yet that all this has been his revenge?

GUIDO: It's your own fault! You don't know how to use the
freedom he's given you.

SILIA: Freedom to let myself be made love to by you or someone else, freedom to stay here or go anywhere I like . . . Oh
yes! I'm free! Free as the air . . . But what if I'm never
myself?

GUIDO: What do you mean, never yourself?

SILIA: Do you really think I'm free to be myself and do just
as I like, as though no one else were there to prevent me?

GUIDO: Well, who is preventing you?

SILIA: *He* is! I can't help seeing him always throwing this
precious freedom to me like an old shoe, and going off to
live by himself – after spending three years proving to me
that this wonderful freedom has no real existence. No matter

18

what use I try to make of it, I shall always be his slave . . .! Even a slave of that chair of his! Look at it: standing in front of me determined to be one of *his* chairs, not something belonging to *me*, and made for *me* to sit in!

GUIDO: This is an obsession, you know.

SILIA: That man haunts me!

GUIDO: You never see him!

SILIA: But he's there, he exists, and I shall always be haunted by him as long as I know he exists. God, I wish he were dead!

GUIDO: Well, he practically is dead as far as you're concerned. He's given up paying you those absurd half-hour visits in the evenings, hasn't he? He only comes as far as the front door and gets the maid to ask if you have any message for him.

SILIA: Yes, but he ought to come up to the flat, and stay here for half an hour every evening. That's what we agreed he was to do.

GUIDO: Really, Silia, this is beyond me. A minute ago you were complaining that . . .

SILIA: Oh, I know to you this is just another of my contradictions!

GUIDO: Well, haven't you just said you were haunted by him?

SILIA: Don't you see it's the fact of his being alive, his mere existence that haunts and obsesses me? It's not his body at all. On the contrary; it would be much better if I did see him. And it's just because he knows that, he doesn't let me see him any more. If he did come in and sit down over there, he'd seem like any other man, neither uglier nor better-looking; I'd see those eyes of his that I never liked (God, they're horrible – sharp as needles and vacant at the same time); I'd hear that voice of his that gets on my nerves; I'd have something tangible to grapple with – and I'd even get some satisfaction out of giving him the bother of coming upstairs for nothing!

GUIDO: I don't believe it.

SILIA: What don't you believe?

GUIDO: That anything could possibly bother him!

SILIA: He's like a ghost, quite detached from life, existing only to haunt other people's lives. I sit for hours on end absolutely crushed by the thought. There he is, alone in his own apartment, dressed up as a cook – (dressed up as a cook, I ask you!) – looking down on everybody from above, watching and understanding every move you make, everything you do, knowing all your thoughts, and making you foresee exactly what you're going to do next – and, of course, when you know what it is, you no longer want to do it! That man has paralysed me! I've only one idea continually gnawing at my brain: how to get rid of him, how to free myself from . . .

[*The house telephone rings off-stage.*]

GUIDO: Really, Silia, aren't you being rather melodramatic!

SILIA: It's the truth.

[*There is a knock at the door on the Left.*]

Come in.

CLARA [*opens the door*]: Excuse me, Signora, the master has rung up from downstairs.

SILIA: Ah, so he's here!

CLARA: He wants to know if there's any message.

SILIA: Yes, there is. Tell him to come up, Clara.

GUIDO: But, Silia . . .

SILIA: Tell him to come up.

CLARA: Very good, Signora. [*She exits.*]

GUIDO: But why, Silia? Why tonight when I'm here?

SILIA: For the very reason that you are here!

GUIDO: No, Silia – don't do it.

SILIA: Yes, I shall – to punish you for coming. What's more I'll leave you here to deal with him. I'm going to my bedroom.

[*She goes towards the door on the Right.*]

GUIDO [*running after her and holding her back*]: No, don't Silia! Are you mad? What will he say?

SILIA: What do you expect him to say?

GUIDO: Silia . . . listen . . . it's late . . .

SILIA: So much the better.

GUIDO: No, no, Silia. That would be going too far. It's madness.

SILIA [*freeing herself from him*]: I don't wish to see him.

GUIDO: Neither do I.

SILIA: You're going to entertain him.

GUIDO: Oh, no, I'm not. He won't find me here either.

[SILIA *goes into her room.* GUIDO *immediately runs into the dining-room, shutting the glass door.*

There is a knock at the front door.]

LEONE [*off*]: May I come in?

[*He opens the door and puts his head round.*]

May I? . . . [*He breaks off, seeing no one there.*]

Well, well!

[*He looks round the room, then takes his watch out of his pocket, goes to the mantelpiece, opens the face of the clock and moves the hands so that it strikes twice, then puts his watch back in his pocket and goes and settles down calmly to await the passing of the agreed half-hour.*

After a short pause a confused whispering is heard from the dining-room. It is SILIA *trying to urge* GUIDO *into the drawing-room.* LEONE *remains motionless. Presently one section of the glass door opens and* GUIDO *enters, leaving the door open.*]

GUIDO [*ill at ease*]: Oh . . . hullo, Leone. I dropped in for a spot of chartreuse.

LEONE: At half-past ten?

GUIDO: Yes . . . As a matter of fact . . . I was just going.

LEONE: I didn't mean that. Was it green chartreuse or yellow?

GUIDO: Oh, I . . . I don't remember. Green, I think.

LEONE: At about two o'clock you'll have the most horrible

nightmare, and wake up with your tongue feeling like a loofah.

GUIDO [*shuddering*]: Oh, don't say that!

LEONE: Yes, you will – result of drinking liqueurs on an empty stomach. Where's Silia?

GUIDO [*embarrassed*]: Well, er . . . she was in there, with me.

LEONE: Where is she now?

GUIDO: I don't know. She . . . she sent me in here when she heard you had come. I expect she'll be . . . joining you soon.

LEONE: Is there something she wants to say to me?

GUIDO: N-no . . . I . . . don't think so.

LEONE: Why did she make me come up, then?

GUIDO: Well, I was just saying good-bye when the maid came in and told her you'd rung up from the hall . . .

LEONE: As I do every evening.

GUIDO: Yes, but . . . apparently she wanted you to come up.

LEONE: Did she say so?

GUIDO: Oh, yes, she said so.

LEONE: Is she angry?

GUIDO: A bit, yes, because . . . I believe that . . . well, I think you two agreed, didn't you? – for the sake of appearances . . .

LEONE: You can leave out the appearances!

GUIDO: I mean, to avoid scandal . . .

LEONE: Scandal?

GUIDO: . . . without going to court.

LEONE: Waste of time!

GUIDO: Well, without openly quarrelling then – you separated.

LEONE: But who on earth would ever quarrel with me? I always give way to everybody.

GUIDO: True. In fact, that's one of your most enviable qualities. But – if I may say so – you go rather too far.

LEONE: You think so?

GUIDO: Yes, because, you see, so often you . . . [*He looks at him and breaks off.*]

LEONE: Well?

GUIDO: You upset people.

LEONE [*amused*]: No! Really? How?

GUIDO: Because . . . you always follow their suggestions. You always do what other people want. I bet that when your wife said to you 'Let's have a judicial separation', you answered . . .

LEONE: 'Very well, let's have a judicial separation.'

GUIDO: There you are, you see! And then when she changed her mind because she didn't want any bother with lawyers and suggested you separated merely by mutual agreement . . .

LEONE: I replied, 'All right, if that's the way you want it, we'll separate by mutual agreement'.

GUIDO: You see? And if, later on, she had come to you and said, 'We can't go on quarrelling like this' . . .

LEONE: . . . I should have said, 'Well then, my dear, we'll not quarrel any more. We'll forget there was ever a difference between us, and start our life together afresh.'

GUIDO: But don't you see that all this is bound to upset people? One gets into the way of behaving as though you didn't exist, and then . . . how can I explain it? However hard one tries to ignore your existence, sooner or later one gets to a point where one can't go any further. It's a dead-end, and one stands there bewildered, because . . . well, it's no use, you *do* exist!

LEONE: Undoubtedly. [*He smiles.*] I exist. [*In a rather sharper tone.*] Ought I *not* to exist?

GUIDO: No, good God, I didn't mean that.

LEONE: But you're right, my dear chap! I ought not to exist. I assure you I do my utmost to exist as little as possible – for my own sake as well as others'. But what can you do? The fault lies with the fact: *I am alive.* And when a fact has happened, it remains there, like a prison, shutting you in. I married Silia, or to be more precise, I let her marry me.

Voilà: another fact! Almost immediately after our wedding, she began to fume and fret, and twist and turn, in her frantic efforts to escape, and I . . . I tell you, Guido, it caused me a great deal of unhappiness. In the end we hit upon this solution. I left her everything here, taking away with me only my books and my pots and pans, which, as you know, are quite indispensable to me. But I realize it's useless because – in name, anyway – the 'part' assigned to me by a fact which cannot be destroyed, remains. I am her husband. That too ought perhaps to be borne occasionally in mind!

[*He pauses.* GUIDO *looks a little uncomfortable.*]

[*Suddenly*] You know what blind people are like, don't you Guido?

GUIDO: Blind people? What do you mean?

LEONE: They are never 'alongside' things, if you understand me.

GUIDO: I don't.

LEONE: If you see a blind man groping for something, and you try to help him by saying 'there it is, just beside you', what does he do? He immediately turns and faces you. It's just the same with that dear woman. She's never by your side – always facing you, opposed to you.

[*He pauses, glancing towards the glass door.*]

It looks as if my wife isn't coming in.

[*He takes his watch out of his pocket: sees that the half-hour is not yet up and puts it back.*]

LEONE: You don't know whether she wanted to say anything to me?

GUIDO: No . . . nothing, I think.

LEONE: In that case, all she wanted was *this*. [*He makes a gesture signifying 'you and me'.*]

GUIDO [*puzzled*]: I don't follow.

LEONE: This situation, my dear chap. She wanted to have the satisfaction of forcing us two to meet like this, face to face.

GUIDO: Perhaps she thinks that I . . .

LEONE: . . . have already gone? No, she would have come in.

GUIDO [*getting ready to go*]: Oh, well, in that case I . . .

LEONE [*quickly, detaining him*]: Oh, no, please don't go. I shall be going in a few minutes. [*He rises.*] Ah, Venanzi, it's a sad thing, when one has learnt every move in the game.

GUIDO: What game?

LEONE: Why . . . this one. The whole game – of life.

GUIDO: Have you learnt it?

LEONE: Yes, a long time ago. And the way to come through it unscathed.

GUIDO: I wish you'd teach me how to do that.

LEONE: Oh, my dear Venanzi, it wouldn't be of any use to you! To get through safe and sound you must know how to defend yourself. But it's a kind of defence that you, probably, wouldn't be able to understand – how shall I describe it? – a desperate one.

GUIDO: How do you mean, desperate? Rash? Reckless?

LEONE: No, no – desperate in the literal sense. Absolutely hopeless – but without the faintest shadow of bitterness, for all that.

GUIDO: Well, what is this defence?

LEONE: It's the firmest and most unshakable of all defences. You see, when there's no more hope left, you're not tempted to make even the slightest concession, either to others or to yourself.

GUIDO: All right. Call it a defence – though I don't see how it can be one. But what is it you're defending?

LEONE [*looks at him severely and darkly for a moment: then, controlling himself, and, as it were, sinking back into an impenetrable serenity*]: The Nothing that lies inside yourself. That is, if you succeed, as I have done, in achieving this nothingness within you. What do you imagine you should defend? Defend yourself, I tell you, against others and above all against yourself; against the injuries life inevitably does to us all; the injury I've done to myself through Silia for so many years; the injury I do to her now, even though I keep myself absolutely isolated like this; the injury you are doing to me . . .

GUIDO: I?

LEONE: Of course – inevitably! [*Looking into his eyes.*] Surely you don't imagine you are not doing me any injury?

GUIDO: Well . . . [*He pales.*] I'm not aware –

LEONE [*encouragingly*]: Oh, unconsciously, of course, my dear Venanzi! When you sit down to eat a roast chicken or a tender veal cutlet, do you ever consider who provides your meal? Are you consciously aware that what you are eating was once a living, breathing, feeling creature? No, you never think about it. Make no mistake, we all injure each other – and each man inures himself, too; naturally! That's life! There's only one thing to do – empty yourself.

GUIDO: Oh, fine! And what's left then?

LEONE: The satisfaction, not of living for yourself any more, but of watching others live – and even of watching yourself, from outside, living that little part of life you are still bound to live.

GUIDO: Only too little, alas!

LEONE: Yes, but you get a marvellous compensation – the thrill of the intellectual game that clears away all the sentimental sediment from your mind, and fixes in calm, precise orbits all that moves tumultuously within you. But the enjoyment of this clear, calm vacuum that you create within you may be dangerous, because, among other things, you run the risk of going up among the clouds like a balloon, unless you put inside yourself the necessary measure of ballast . . .

GUIDO: Oh, I see! By eating well?

LEONE [*ignoring the interjection*]: To re-establish your equilibrium, so that you will always stay upright. You know those celluloid toys? – those funny little hollow figures you give to children to play with? You can knock them over any way you like, and they always spring up again. That's because of their lead counter-weight. I assure you we're very much the same as they are. Only you have to learn how to make yourself hollow, and – more important – how to provide yourself with a counter-weight.

GUIDO: I don't follow you.

LEONE: No, I feared you wouldn't. To put it more concisely – you can ride out the storms of life only if you are securely anchored. Find yourself an anchor, then, my dear Venanzi – some hobby, some absorbing mental occupation, some fanciful conceit – then you'll be safe.

GUIDO: Oh, no, no! Thanks very much! That sort of thing is not for me. It sounds much too difficult.

LEONE: It's not easy, I grant you; because you can't buy these anchors ready made. You have to make them for yourself – and not just one, either. You need many anchors, one to suit each emergency, every incident in life. And, too, they must be stout and strong, to stand the strain of any violent incident that may burst upon you without warning.

GUIDO: Yes, but surely there are certain unforeseen incidents, sometimes really shattering ones, that even you can't –

LEONE: – That's just where my cooking comes in. It's wonderful what storms you can weather if you're a good cook.

GUIDO: Really?

LEONE: In any case, it's never really the incident itself you have to consider. After all, what does 'incident' imply? The activity of other people, or an act of God.

GUIDO: Precisely, and they can both be terrible.

LEONE: But more or less terrible according to the person who experiences them. That's why I say you must defend yourself against yourself – against the feelings immediately aroused in you by anything that happens to you – the feelings which are, in reality, the weapons the incident uses in its attack upon you. The best defence is counter-attack, you know. You must grapple with the incident without hesitation, before it gets a chance to engage your feelings, and get out of it anything that may be of advantage to you. The residue will be powerless to injure you, you can laugh at it, play with it, make it the fanciful conceit I mentioned just now.

GUIDO [*more and more bewildered*]: I'm afraid I still don't quite . . .

LEONE: Look, Venanzi. Imagine for a moment that you suddenly notice an egg hurtling through the air straight towards you –

GUIDO: – An egg?

LEONE: Yes, an egg. A fresh one. It doesn't matter who has thrown it, or where it comes from; that's beside the point.

GUIDO: But suppose it turns out to be a bullet and not an egg?

LEONE [*smiling*]: Then it's too late to think about emptying yourself. The bullet will do the job for you, and that's the end of the matter.

GUIDO: All right – let's stick to your egg; although what a fresh egg has to do with the matter, I'm blessed if I can see.

LEONE: To give you a fresh image of events and ideas. Well, now, if you're not prepared to catch the egg, what happens? Either you stand still and the egg hits you and smashes, or you duck and it misses you and smashes on the ground. In either case the result is a wasted egg. But if you are prepared, you catch it, and then – why, there's no end to what you can do with it, if you're a good cook. You can boil it, or poach it, or fry it, or make an omelet out of it. Or you can simply pierce it at each end and suck out the yolk. What's left in your hand then?

GUIDO: The empty shell.

LEONE: There you have the idea. That empty shell is your fanciful conceit. You can amuse yourself with it by sticking it on a pin and making it spin; or you can toss it from one hand to the other like a ping-pong ball. When you're tired of playing with it, what do you do? You crush it in your hands and throw it away.

[*At this point* SILIA, *in the dining-room, suddenly laughs loudly.*]

SILIA [*hiding behind the closed section of the glass door*]: But I'm not an empty egg-shell in your hand.

LEONE [*turning quickly and going to the door*]: No, dear; and you no longer come through the air towards *me* for *me* to catch.

[*He has hardly finished saying this when* SILIA, *without showing herself, shuts the other half-door in his face.* LEONE *stands there for a moment, nodding. Then he comes forward again and turns to* GUIDO.]

That's a great misfortune for me, my dear Venanzi. She was a wonderful school of experience. I've come to miss her. She is full of unhappiness because she's full of life. Not one life only, many. But there isn't one of them that will ever give her an anchor. There's no salvation for her – [*pointedly*] And so there's no peace . . . either for her, or with her.

[GUIDO, *absorbed in thought, unconsciously nods too, with a sad expression on his face.*]

You agree?

GUIDO [*thoughtfully*]: Yes . . . it's perfectly true.

LEONE: You're probably unaware of all the riches there are in her . . . qualities of mind and spirit you would never believe to be hers – because you've studied only one facet of her character, from which you have built up your idea of what is for you, and always will be, the real and only Silia. You'd think it impossible, for example, for Silia to go about her housework some morning carefree, relaxed, happily singing and humming to herself. But she does, you know. I used to hear her sometimes, going from room to room singing in a sweet little quavering voice, like a child's. A different woman. I'm not saying that just for the sake of saying it. Really a different woman – without knowing it! For a few moments when she is out of herself, she is just

a child, singing. And if you could see how she sits sometimes, absorbed, gazing into space; a distant, living glow
reflected in her eyes, and unconsciously smoothing her hair
with idly straying fingers. Who is she then? Not the Silia
you know – another Silia, a Silia that can't live because she
is unknown to herself, since no one has ever said to her: 'I
love you when you are like that; that's the way I want you
always to be.' If you told her that, she'd ask you, 'How do
you want me to be?' You would reply, 'As you were just
now'. Then she would turn to you, 'What was I like,' she
would say, 'what was I doing?' 'You were singing.' 'I was
singing?' 'Yes, and you were smoothing your hair like this.'
She would not know it; she would tell you it wasn't true.
She positively would not recognize herself in your picture
of her as you had just seen her – if you *could* see her like that,
for you always see only one side of her! How sad it is,
Guido! Here's a sweet, gracious potentiality of a life she
might have – and she hasn't got it!

[*A sad pause. In the silence, the ormolu clock strikes eleven.*]
Ah, eleven o'clock. Say good night to her for me.

SILIA [*quickly opening the glass door*]: Wait – wait a minute.

LEONE: Oh, no. The half-hour is up.

SILIA: I wanted to give you this.

[*She puts an egg-shell into his hand, laughing.*]

LEONE: Oh, but *I* haven't sucked it! Here . . .

[*He goes quickly to* GUIDO *and gives him the egg-shell.*]
Let's give it to Guido!

[GUIDO *automatically takes the egg-shell, and stands stupidly
with it in his hand, while* LEONE, *laughing loudly, goes off
through the door on the Left.*]

SILIA: I'd give anything for someone to kill him!

GUIDO: I'd love to chuck this egg at his head.

[*He runs towards the window on the Left.*]

SILIA [*laughing*]: Here, give it to me! I'll throw it at him from
the window.

[GUIDO *gives her the egg-shell, or rather lets her take it from him.*]

GUIDO: Will you be able to hit him?

SILIA: Yes, as he comes out of the front door.

[*She leans out of the window, looking down, ready to throw the egg-shell.*]

GUIDO [*behind her*]: Careful.

[SILIA *throws the shell, then suddenly draws back with an exclamation of dismay.*]

What have you done?

SILIA: Oh, Lord!

GUIDO: Did you hit someone else?

SILIA: Yes. The wind made it swerve.

GUIDO: Naturally! It was empty. Trust a woman not to allow for the wind!

SILIA: They are coming up.

GUIDO: Who's coming up.

SILIA: There were four men talking by the door. They were coming in just as he went out. Perhaps they are tenants.

GUIDO: Well, what does it matter, anyway?

[*He takes advantage of her consternation and kisses her.*]

SILIA: It looks as though it landed on one of them.

GUIDO: But an empty egg-shell couldn't possibly hurt him! Forget about it! [*Recalling Leone's words, but passionately and without caricature*] You know, darling, you are just like a child.

SILIA: What *are* you saying?

GUIDO: You are like a child tonight, and I love you when you're like that. That's the way I want you always to be.

SILIA [*laughs*]: You're repeating what *he* said.

GUIDO [*not put off by her laughter, but still passionately, his desire increasing*]: Yes, I know I am, but it's true, it's true! Can't you see you're just a wayward child?

SILIA: A child? [*Raising her hands to his face, as though to scratch him.*] More likely a tigress!

GUIDO [*without letting her go*]: For him, perhaps, but not for me. I love you so. To me you're a child.

SILIA [*half-laughing*]: All right, then, you kill him for me!

GUIDO: Oh, darling, do be serious.

SILIA: Well, if I'm a child I can ask you to do that for me, can't I?

GUIDO [*playing up*]: Because he's your 'bogeyman'?

SILIA: Yes, he's the 'bogeyman' who makes me so frightened. Will you kill him for me?

GUIDO: Yes, yes, I'll kill him . . . but not now, later. Now I want to . . .

[*He clasps her more closely.*]

SILIA [*struggling*]: No, no! Guido, please . . .

GUIDO: Oh, Silia, you must know how much I love you; how I long for you!

SILIA [*as before, but languidly*]: No, I tell you

GUIDO [*trying to lead her towards the door on the Right*]: Yes, yes! Come, Silia.

SILIA: No. Please! Leave me!

GUIDO: How can I leave you now, darling?

SILIA: No, Guido, no! Not in the flat! I shouldn't like the maid to . . .

[*There is a knock on the door, Left.*]

There, you see?

GUIDO: Don't let her in. I'll wait for you in your room.

[*He goes towards the door on the Right.*]

But don't be long.

[*He exits, shutting the door.*

SILIA *goes to the other door, but before she reaches it,* CLARA *is heard shouting outside.*]

CLARA: Take your hands off me. Go away! She doesn't live here!

[*The door bursts open and* MARQUIS MIGLIORITI *with three other 'young-men-about-town', all in evening dress and drunk, lurch in, pushing forward. She is still trying to prevent their entry.*]

MIGLIORITI: Out of the way, you old owl. What do you mean by saying she doesn't live here, when she's here all the time?

1ST DRUNK: Lovely Pepita! The gay señorita!

2ND DRUNK: Viva España. Viva España.

3RD DRUNK [*not so stupidly drunk as the others*]: I say, fellows: just look at this flat! C'est tout à fait charmant!

SILIA [*to* CLARA]: What's the meaning of this? Who are they? How did they get in?

CLARA: They forced their way in, Signora. They're drunk.

MIGLIORITI [*to* CLARA]: Some force, eh! You old owl!

1ST DRUNK: Some drunks!

2ND DRUNK: Gorgeously drunk drunks!

MIGLIORITI: But you invited me, Señorita! [*This to* SILIA.] You dropped an egg-shell on me from the window!

2ND DRUNK: D'you know what we are? We are four gentlemen!

1ST DRUNK: Caballeros!

3RD DRUNK [*pointing to the dining-room and then going into it*]: I wonder if a client gets a drink here? [*He notices the decanters on the table.*] Ah, we're in luck! C'est tout à fait délicieux!

SILIA [*noting the implications of the word 'client'*]: Good Lord! What do they want?

CLARA [*to* MIGLIORITI]: How dare you! This is a respectable house!

MIGLIORITI: But of course, we know that. [*To* SILIA] Charming Pepita!

SILIA: Pepita!?

CLARA: Yes, Signorina . . . that woman next door. I kept telling them this wasn't her flat.

SILIA [*bursts out laughing. Then with a sinister light in her eyes, as though a diabolical idea has come into her head, she says*]: Why, yes, of course, gentlemen, I am Pepita.

2ND DRUNK: Viva España. Viva Pepita!

SILIA [to all three]: Do sit down, won't you? Or perhaps you'd rather join your friend in there for a drink?

MIGLIORITI [attempting to kiss her]: No, I . . . well, really . . . I'd rather . . .

SILIA [evades him]: Rather what?

MIGLIORITI: I'd rather drink you first!

SILIA: Wait! Wait a moment!

2ND DRUNK [imitating MIGLIORITI'S actions]: Me too, Pepita!

SILIA [warding him off]: You too? All right . . . steady now.

2ND DRUNK: What we want is an ab-sho-lutely Spanish night!

1ST DRUNK: Personally, I don't actually propose to do anything, but . . .

SILIA: Yes, all right . . . all right . . . steady now. Now come and sit down over here, boys.

[She frees herself and pushes them towards chairs, making them sit down.]

That's right . . . fine! That's it.

[They mutter among themselves. SILIA runs to CLARA and whispers]

SILIA: Go upstairs and fetch some of the neighbours. Downstairs too. Hurry!

[CLARA nods and runs off.

GUIDO starts to open the bedroom door.]

SILIA [to MIGLIORITI and the others]: Excuse me a minute . . .

[She goes to the door on the Right and locks it to prevent GUIDO from coming in.]

MIGLIORITI [trying to get up]: Oh, if you've got a gentleman in there already, carry on you know, don't mind us!

2ND DRUNK: No, don't mind us, carry on – carry on – we don't mind waiting!

1ST DRUNK: Personally, I don't actually propose to do anything but . . . [He tries to get up.]

SILIA [to MIGLIORITI and the 1ST DRUNK]: Don't get up!

Stay where you are. [*To all three*] Listen – you gentlemen are quite . . . I mean, you know what you are doing, don't you?

ALL: Of course! Absolutely. Of course we do. Why shouldn't we? Know what we're doing, indeed!

SILIA: And you don't for a moment suspect that you are in a respectable house, do you?

3RD DRUNK [*staggering in from the dining-room with a glass in his hand*]: Oh, oui . . . mais . . . n'exagère pas, mon petit chou! Nous voulons nous amuser un peu . . . Voilà tout!

SILIA: But I am at home only to friends. Now, if you want to be friends . . .

2ND DRUNK: Mais certainement!

1ST DRUNK: Intimate friends! [*He tries to rise and bow.*] [*He subsides muttering 'Dear little Pepita! Lovely little Pepita!' etc.*]

SILIA: Then please tell me your names.

2ND DRUNK: My name is Coco.

SILIA: No . . . not like that . . .

2ND DRUNK: Honestly, my name is Coco.

1ST DRUNK: And mine is Meme.

SILIA: No, no! I mean, will you give me your visiting cards?

2ND DRUNK: Oh no, no, no! Thank you very much, sweetheart.

1ST DRUNK: I haven't got one . . . I've lost my pocket-book . . . [*To* MIGLIORITI] Be a good chap, and give her one for me.

SILIA [*sweetly – to* MIGLIORITI]: Yes, you're the nicest. You'll give me yours, won't you?

MIGLIORITI [*taking out his pocket-book*]: Certainly – I have no objection.

2ND DRUNK: He can give you cards for all of us . . . voilà!

MIGLIORITI: Here you are, Pepita.

SILIA: Oh, thank you. Good. [*Reading it.*] So you are Marquis Miglioriti?

1ST DRUNK [*laughing*]: That's right – he's a Marquis . . . But only a little one!

SILIA [*to* 2ND DRUNK]: And you are Meme?

1ST DRUNK: No, I'm Meme. [*Pointing to* 2ND DRUNK] He's Coco.

SILIA: Oh yes, of course: Coco – Meme. [*To the* 3RD DRUNK] And you?

3RD DRUNK [*with a silly, sly look*]: Moi? Moi . . . je ne sais pas, mon petit chou.

SILIA: Well, it doesn't matter. One is enough.

2ND DRUNK: But we all want to be in it. We all want –

3RD DRUNK: – an absolutely Spanish night!

1ST DRUNK: Personally, I don't actually propose to do anything . . . but I should love to see you dance, Pepita . . . you know, with castanets . . . Ta-trrrra-ti-ta-ti, ta-trrrra-ti-ta-ti . . .

2ND DRUNK: Yes, yes. Dance first . . . and *then* . . .

MIGLIORITI: But not dressed like that!

3RD DRUNK: Why dressed at all, gentlemen?

2ND DRUNK [*rising and staggering right up to* SILIA]: Yes, that's right! Without a stitch!

[MIGLIORITI *and the others crowd round* SILIA *as if to strip her.*]

ALL: Yes, stripped . . . in the altogether. That's the idea! Splendid! Without a stitch. Splendid!

SILIA [*freeing herself*]: But not in here, gentlemen, please. Naked, if you like. But not here.

3RD DRUNK: Where then?

SILIA: Down in the square.

MIGLIORITI [*standing still, sobering up a little*]: In the square?

1ST DRUNK [*quietly*]: Naked in the square?

SILIA: Of course! Why not? It's the ideal place. The moon is shining – there won't be anyone about . . . just the statue of the king on horseback – and you four gentlemen . . . in evening dress.

[*At this point* THREE MEN *and* TWO WOMEN – *tenants of the floors above and below – rush in with* CLARA, *shouting confusedly*.]

THE TENANTS: What's the matter? What's happened? Who are they? What's going on here? What have they done to her? Has she been assaulted?

CLARA: There they are! There they are!

SILIA [*suddenly changing her tone and demeanour*]: I've been assaulted! Assaulted in my own home! They forced their way in, knocked me down, and pulled me about, as you can see, and they've molested me and insulted me in every possible way, the cowards!

2ND TENANT [*trying to chase them out*]: Get out of here! Get out!

1ST TENANT: Stand back! Leave her alone!

3RD TENANT: Come along! Get out of here!

1ST DRUNK: All right! Keep calm! Keep calm!

2ND TENANT: Go on! Get out!

1ST WOMAN TENANT: What scoundrels.

MIGLIORITI: Well, this is an open house, isn't it? Anybody can come in, surely?

1ST DRUNK: Spain is doing a brisk trade!

2ND WOMAN TENANT: Well . . . Really!!!

1ST WOMAN TENANT: Get out, you disgusting drunken lot, you!

3RD DRUNK: Oh, I say, there's no need to make such a fuss, you know.

MIGLIORITI: Dear Pepita . . .

2ND TENANT: What, Pepita?

1ST WOMAN TENANT: Pepita! This isn't Pepita, young man. This is Signora Gala.

3RD TENANT: Of course. Signora Gala.

MIGLIORITI AND THE THREE DRUNKS: Signora Gala.

3RD DRUNK: Not Pepita?

1ST TENANT: Certainly not! Signora Gala.

1ST WOMAN TENANT: You ought to be ashamed of yourselves. Good for nothing, drunken hooligans, that's what
you are!

2ND DRUNK: Oh, well . . . in that case, we'll apologize to the
Signora for our mistake.

ALL THE TENANTS: Go along, now! Get out! Leave this place
at once!

1ST DRUNK: Doucement . . . doucement, s'il vous plaît!

2ND DRUNK: We thought she was Pepita.

3RD DRUNK: Yes, and we wanted to do homage to
Spain. To-re-ador, tum, tum-ti, tumti, tummm . . . [*He
starts to sing the aria from* Carmen.]

3RD TENANT: That's quite enough, now! Get out!

2ND DRUNK: No! First we must beg the Signora's pardon.

1ST TENANT: Stop it. That'll do now. Go home.

MIGLIORITI: Yes – very well. But, look here, all of you, look
here. [*He kneels in front of* SILIA.] Down on our knees, we
offer you our humble apologies.

ALL DRUNKS: That's right . . . on our knees. Go on, Coco . . .
down you go . . . etc.

SILIA: Oh, no! That's not good enough. Marquis, I have your
name, and you and your friends will have to answer for the
outrage you have done to me in my own home.

MIGLIORITI: But Signora – if we beg your pardon . . .

SILIA: I accept no apologies.

MIGLIORITI [*rising, much sobered*]: Very well. You have my
card . . . and I'm quite ready to answer –

SILIA: Now get out of my flat – at once!

[*The* FOUR DRUNKS, *who nevertheless feel compelled to bow,
are driven out by the* TENANTS, *and accompanied to the door
by* CLARA.]

[*To the* TENANTS]: Thank you all very much indeed. I'm
awfully sorry to have bothered you all.

2ND TENANT: Not at all, Signora Gala.

1ST TENANT: Don't mention it.

1ST WOMAN TENANT: After all, we're neighbours – and if neighbours don't help each other . . .

2ND TENANT: What scoundrels!

1ST WOMAN TENANT: We can't be safe even in our homes these days.

2ND TENANT: But perhaps, Signora Gala – seeing that they begged your pardon . . .

SILIA: Oh, no! They were told several times that this was a respectable place, and in spite of that . . . Really, you wouldn't believe what an improper suggestion they dared to make to me.

1ST TENANT: Yes, you were quite right to take no excuses, Signora Gala.

2ND TENANT: Oh, you've done the right thing, there's no doubt about that.

THE WOMEN TENANTS: They must be given a good lesson. You poor dear! Horsewhipping would be too good for them.

SILIA: I know the name of one of them. He gave me his card.

3RD TENANT: Who is he?

SILIA [*showing the card*]: Marquis Aldo Miglioriti.

1ST WOMAN TENANT: Oh! Marquis Miglioriti!

2ND WOMAN TENANT: A Marquis!

ALL: He ought to be ashamed of himself! Disgraceful! A Marquis to behave like that! That makes his behaviour all the worse! etc.

SILIA: You agree then that I had every right to be annoyed?

2ND WOMAN TENANT: Oh, yes! You're perfectly justified in teaching them a lesson, Signora Gala.

1ST WOMAN TENANT: They must be shown up, Signora. Shown up!

2ND TENANT: And punished!

1ST TENANT: They ought to be publicly disgraced!

2ND TENANT: But don't be too upset, Signora Gala.

2ND WOMAN TENANT: You ought to rest a little.

1ST WOMAN TENANT: Yes – it would do you good . . . after such an experience!

2ND WOMAN TENANT: Yes, we'll leave you now, dear.

ALL TENANTS: Good night, Signora Gala . . . etc.

[*Exeunt.*

As soon as the TENANTS *have gone,* SILIA *looks radiantly at* MIGLIORITI'S *card, and nods to herself, laughing, to indicate that she has achieved her secret object. Meanwhile* GUIDO *is hammering on the door Right, with his fists.*]

SILIA: All right! All right! All right! I'm coming!

[SILIA *runs and unlocks the door.* GUIDO ENTERS, *trembling with rage and indignation.*]

GUIDO: Why did you lock me in? I was longing to get my hands on their throats. My God, if I could have got at those ruffians!

SILIA: Oh, yes, that's right! It only needed you to come dashing to my defence out of my bedroom, to compromise me and . . . [*with a mad glint in her eyes*] . . . spoil everything! [*Showing him Miglioriti's card.*] Look. I've got it. I've got it!

GUIDO: What?

SILIA: One of their visiting cards!

GUIDO [*reading it – with surprise*]: Marquis Miglioriti? I know him well. But what do you propose to do?

SILIA: I've got it, and I'm going to give it to my husband!

GUIDO: To Leone? [*He looks at her in terrified astonishment.*] But, Silia . . .!

[*He tries to take the card from her.*]

SILIA [*preventing him*]: I want to see if I can't cause him . . . [*sarcastically*] just the 'slightest little bit of bother'.

GUIDO: But do you realize who this man is?

SILIA: Marquis Aldo Miglioriti.

GUIDO: Silia, listen to me! For goodness' sake get this idea out of your head.

SILIA: I'll do nothing of the sort. *You* needn't worry. He'll

40

realize that my lover couldn't possibly have come forward to defend me.

GUIDO: No, no, Silia, I tell you. You mustn't! I'll stop you at all costs!

SILIA: You'll stop nothing! In the first place, you can't . . .

GUIDO: Yes I can, and will! You'll see!

SILIA: We'll see about that tomorrow. [*Imperiously.*] I've had enough of this. I'm tired.

GUIDO [*in a threatening tone*]: Very well. I'm going.

SILIA [*imperiously*]: No! [*She pauses, then – changing her tone of voice*] Come here, Guido!

GUIDO [*not altering his attitude, but going nearer to her*]: What do you want?

SILIA: I want . . . I want you to stop being such a silly spoil-sport.

[*Pause. She laughs to herself.*]

Those poor boys! You know, I really did treat them rather badly.

GUIDO: As a matter of fact you did. After all, they admitted they'd made a mistake. And they begged your pardon.

SILIA [*curt and imperious again, not wishing to admit any discussion on this point*]: That'll do, I tell you. I don't want to hear any more about that. I'm thinking of how funny they looked, poor boys. [*With a sigh of heartfelt envy.*] Such wonderful fantasies men get hold of at night. What fun they have! Moonlight, and . . . Do you know, Guido, they wanted to see me dance . . . in the square . . . [*Very softly, almost in his ear*] Naked.

GUIDO: Silia!

SILIA [*leaning her head back and tickling his face with her hair*]: Guido . . . do you remember you called me a wayward child? [*Seductively*] I want to be your wayward child.

GUIDO [*embracing her*]: Silia . . .

ACT TWO

A room in LEONE GALA'*s flat.*

It is an unusual room, fitted up to be at the same time a dining-room and a study. There is a dining-table laid for lunch – and a writing-desk covered with books, papers, and writing material. There are glass-fronted cabinets filled with sumptuous silver epergnes and cruets, a fine porcelain dinner service, and valuable wine-glasses – and book-shelves lined with solid-looking volumes. In fact, all the furniture accentuates the dual function of the room, with the exception of a third, occasional table on which there are a vase of flowers, a cigar-box, and an ash-tray.

At the back, a door connects this room with LEONE'*s bedroom.*

To the Left, a door leads to the kitchen.

To the Right is the main door into the room from the hall.

The time is the next morning.

[*When the curtain rises,* LEONE, *in cook's cap and apron, is busy beating an egg in a bowl with a wooden spoon.* PHILIP, *also dressed as a cook, is beating another.* GUIDO VENANZI, *seated, is listening to* LEONE.]

LEONE: Yes, my dear Venanzi, he's so rude to me sometimes: you must wonder why I put up with him.

PHILIP [*surly and bored*]: Don't talk so much – and carry on beating that egg.

LEONE: Do you hear that, Venanzi? Anyone would think he was the master and I the servant. But he amuses me. Philip is my 'tame devil'.

PHILIP: I wish the devil would fly away with you.

LEONE: Tt Tt . . . now he's swearing. You see? I can hardly talk to him!

PHILIP: There's no need to talk. Keep quiet.

[LEONE *laughs.*]

GUIDO: Really, Socrates!

PHILIP: Now, don't *you* start calling me Socrates. I've had enough of it from the master. To hell with Socrates. I don't even know who he is.

LEONE: What! [*laughing*] You don't know him?

PHILIP: No, Signore! And I don't want to have anything to do with him. Keep an eye on that egg.

LEONE: All right! I'm watching it.

PHILIP: How are you beating it?

LEONE: With a spoon, of course.

PHILIP: Yes, yes! But which side of the spoon are you using?

LEONE: Oh, the back: don't worry!

PHILIP: You'll poison that gentleman at lunch, I tell you, if you don't stop chattering.

GUIDO: No, no, Philip. Let him go on. I'm enjoying myself.

LEONE: I'm emptying him out of himself a bit, to give him an appetite.

PHILIP: But you're disturbing *me*.

LEONE [*laughing*]: And 'me' is the only one who matters! Now we've come to the point!

PHILIP: You've hit it. What are you doing now?

LEONE: What am I doing?

PHILIP: Go on beating that egg, for goodness' sake! You mustn't slacken or you'll ruin it

LEONE: All right, all right!

PHILIP: Have I got to keep my eyes on what he's doing, my ears on what he's saying, and my mind – that's already in a whirl – on all the tomfoolery that comes out of his mouth? I'm off to the kitchen!

LEONE: No, Philip – don't be a fool. Stay here. I'll be quiet. [*To* GUIDO, *sotto voce, but so that* PHILIP *can hear*] He used not to be like this. Bergson has done for him.

PHILIP: Now he's trotting out that Bergson!

LEONE: Yes, and why not? [*To* GUIDO] D'you know, Venanzi, since I expounded to him Bergson's theory of

intuition, he's become a different man. He used to be a
powerful thinker . . .

PHILIP: I've never been a thinker, for your information! And
if you go on like this, I'll drop everything here and leave
you, once and for all. Then you'll be properly in the soup!

LEONE [to GUIDO]: You see? And I'm not allowed to say
Bergson has ruined him! Mark you, I quite agree with what
you say about his views on reason . . .

PHILIP: Well, if you agree there's nothing more to be said!
Beat that egg!

LEONE: I'm beating it, I'm beating it! But listen a moment:
according to Bergson, anything in reality that is fluid,
living, mobile, and indeterminate lies beyond the scope of
reason . . . [To GUIDO, as though in parenthesis] though how
it manages to escape reason, I don't know, seeing that
Bergson is able to say it does. What makes him say so if it
isn't his reason? And in that case, it seems to me it can't be
beyond reason. What do you say?

PHILIP: Beat that egg! [He is exasperated.]

LEONE: I am beating it, can't you see? Listen, Venanzi . . .

GUIDO: Oh, do stop calling me by my surname. Everyone
calls me Guido.

LEONE [with a strange smile]: I prefer to think of you as
Venanzi. Anyway, listen: it's a fine game reason plays with
Bergson, making him think she has been dethroned and
slighted by him, to the infinite delight of all the feather-
brained philosophizing females in Paris! He maintains that
reason can consider only the identical and constant aspects
and characteristics of matter. She has geometrical and
mechanical habits. Reality is a ceaseless flow of perpetual
newness, which reason breaks down into so many static
and homogeneous particles . . .

[During this speech, LEONE, as he gets worked up, gradually
forgets his egg-beating, and finally stops. PHILIP, always watching him and beating his own egg, approaches him stealthily.]

PHILIP [*leaning forward and almost shouting at him*]: And what are you doing now?

LEONE [*with a start, beginning to beat again*]: Right you are! I'm beating the egg! Look!

PHILIP: You're not concentrating! All this talk about reason is taking your mind off what you're supposed to be doing.

LEONE: How impatient you are, my dear fellow! I'm perfectly well aware of the necessity of beating eggs. [*Beating rapidly.*] As you see, I accept and obey this necessity. But am I not allowed to use my mind for anything else?

GUIDO [*laughing*]: You really are wonderful! The pair of you!

LEONE: No, no! You're wrong there! I'm wonderful if you like. But *he*, for a long time now – since he has been corrupted by Bergson, in fact –

PHILIP: No one has corrupted me, if you don't mind!

LEONE: Oh, yes, my dear chap! You've become so deplorably human that I don't recognize you any more.

[PHILIP *is about to remonstrate.*]

LEONE: Do let me finish what I'm saying, for goodness' sake! We must have a little more emptiness to make room for all this batter. Look! I've filled the bowl with my energetic beating!

[*There is a loud ring at the front door.* PHILIP *puts down his bowl and goes towards the door on the Right.*]

LEONE [*putting down his bowl*]: Wait. Wait. Come here. Untie this apron for me first.

[PHILIP *does so.*]

And take this into the kitchen too. [*He takes off his cap and gives it to* PHILIP.]

PHILIP: You've done it an honour, I must say!

[*He goes off to the Left, leaves the apron and cap in the kitchen, and returns a moment later, during the ensuing conversation between* LEONE *and* GUIDO, *to collect the two bowls of batter and take them into the kitchen. He forgets to answer the bell.*]

GUIDO [*who has got up, very worried and perplexed at the sound of the bell*]: Did . . . did someone ring?

LEONE [*noting his perturbation*]: Yes. Why? What's the matter?

GUIDO: Good God – Leone, it must be Silia!

LEONE: Silia? Here?

GUIDO: Yes. Listen, for Heaven's sake. I came early like this, to tell you . . . [*He hesitates.*]

LEONE: What?

GUIDO: About something that happened last night . . .

LEONE: To Silia?

GUIDO: Yes, but it's nothing, really. Just something rather silly. That's why I haven't said anything to you. I hoped that after sleeping on it she would have forgotten the whole thing.

[*Renewed, louder ringing at the door.*]

GUIDO: But there she is – that must be Silia!

LEONE [*calmly, turning towards the door on the Left*]: Socrates! For goodness' sake go and open the door!

GUIDO: Just a minute. [*To* PHILIP, *as he enters*] Wait! [*To* LEONE] I warn you, Leone, that your wife intends to do something really crazy . . .

LEONE: That's nothing new!

GUIDO: . . . at *your* expense. She wants to make you suffer for it.

LEONE: Make me suffer, eh? [*To* PHILIP] Let her in. Go and open the door! [*To* GUIDO] My dear Venanzi, my wife is always sure of a welcome, when she comes to visit me on that sort of business!

[PHILIP, *more irritated than ever, goes to open the door.*]

GUIDO: But you don't know what it's about!

LEONE: It doesn't matter what it's about! Let her go ahead! You'll see! Remember what I do with the egg? I catch it, I pierce it, and I suck the yolk out of it!

SILIA [*entering like a whirlwind and seeing* GUIDO]: Oh, so you're here, Guido! I suppose you came to warn him.

46

GUIDO: No, Silia. I swear I haven't said a word to him!

SILIA [*looking closely at* LEONE]: I can see he knows.

LEONE: No, dear. I don't know anything. [*Assuming a light, gay tone.*] Good morning!

SILIA [*quivering with rage*]: Good morning, indeed! If you've told him Guido, I'll never –

LEONE: No, no, Silia. You can say what you've come to say, without any fear of losing the effect of complete surprise you've been looking forward to. He's told me nothing. However, go out if you like, and make your entry again, in order to come upon me unexpectedly.

SILIA: Look here, Leone, I've not come here for fun! [*To* GUIDO] What are you doing here, then?

GUIDO: Well, I came . . .

LEONE: Tell her the truth. He came to warn me, sure enough, of some crazy plan or other of yours.

SILIA [*exploding*]: Crazy plan, you call it!

GUIDO: Yes, Silia. Personally, I can't consider it anything else.

LEONE: But he hasn't told me. I don't know what it is.

GUIDO: I hoped you wouldn't come here –

LEONE: – So he didn't say a word about it, you see!

SILIA: How do you know it's 'one of my crazy plans', then?

LEONE: Oh, that I could imagine for myself. But really –

GUIDO: Yes, I did tell him that much – that it was a crazy plan! And I stick to it!

SILIA [*exasperated to the utmost*]: Will you keep quiet! No one has given you the right to criticize the way I feel about things! [*She pauses, then, turning to* LEONE, *as though shooting him in the chest.*] You've been challenged!

LEONE: What? I've been challenged?

GUIDO: Impossible!

SILIA: Yes, you have.

LEONE: Who has challenged me?

GUIDO: It's impossible, I tell you.

SILIA: Well, I don't really know whether he's challenged you, or whether you have to challenge him. I don't understand these things. But I do know that I've got the wretched man's card . . . [*She takes it out of her bag.*] Here it is. [*She gives it to* LEONE.] You must get dressed at once, and go and find two seconds.

LEONE: Hold on. Not so fast!

SILIA: No, you must do it now. Don't pay any attention to what *he* says! He only wants to make you think this is 'one of my crazy plans' because that would suit him!

LEONE: Oh, it would suit him, would it?

GUIDO [*furiously indignant*]: What do you mean?

SILIA: Of course it suits you to put that idea into his head. Otherwise you'd still be making the same excuses for that . . . that scoundrel!

LEONE [*looking at the card*]: Who is he?

GUIDO: Marquis Aldo Miglioriti.

LEONE: Do you know him?

GUIDO: Very well indeed. He's one of the best swordsmen in town.

SILIA: Ah, so that's why!

GUIDO [*pale, quavering*]: That's why what? What do you mean?

SILIA [*as though to herself, scornfully, disdainfully*]: That's why! That's why!

LEONE: Well, at any rate, am I going to be allowed to know what's happened? Why should I be challenged? Or why should I challenge anybody?

SILIA [*in a rush*]: Because I've been insulted, and outraged, and indecently assaulted – in my own home, too! And all through you – because I was alone and defenceless! Grossly insulted! They put their hands on me, and mauled me about – [*touching her breast*] here, do you understand? Because they thought I was . . . Oh! [*She covers her face with her hands and breaks out into harsh, convulsive sobs of shame and rage.*]

LEONE: But I don't understand – did this Marquis . . .

SILIA: There were four of them. You saw them yourself as you were leaving the house.

LEONE: Oh, those four men who were by the front door?

SILIA: Yes. They came up and forced the door.

GUIDO: But they were tight. They didn't know what they were doing!

LEONE: Hallo! What's this? Were you still there?

[*This question, heavy with mock astonishment, puts* SILIA *and* GUIDO *at a loss. There is a pause.*]

GUIDO: Yes . . . but . . . I wasn't . . .

SILIA [*suddenly plucking up her courage again – aggressively*]: Why should he have protected me? Was it his job to do so when my husband had just that very moment turned his back, leaving me exposed to the attack of four ruffians, who – if Guido had come forward . . .

GUIDO [*interrupting*]: I was in the . . . next room, you see, and –

SILIA: – In the dining-room –

LEONE [*very calmly*]: Having another liqueur?

SILIA [*in a furious outburst*]: But do you know what they said to me? They said: 'If you've got a gentleman in there, carry on, don't mind us.' It only needed him to show himself, for me to be finally compromised! Thank goodness he had sense enough to realize that and keep out of sight!

LEONE: I understand, I understand! But I am surprised, Silia – more than surprised – absolutely amazed, to find that your pretty little head could ever have been capable of such clear discernment!

SILIA [*tonelessly, not understanding*]: What discernment?

LEONE: Why, that it was up to *me* to protect you, because, after all, I am your husband, while Venanzi here . . . if he had attempted to stop those four drunks . . . by the way, he must have been more than a little tight himself . . .

GUIDO: Tight! I tell you I didn't come in because I thought it more discreet not to!

LEONE: And you were quite right not to, my dear chap!
What is so wonderful is that that pretty little head was able
to understand that 'discretion' of yours, and could grasp
that you would have compromised her if you had shown
yourself – so she didn't call you to her aid, though she was
being attacked by four hooligans!

SILIA [*quickly almost childishly*]: They were crowding round
me, all of them, clutching at me and trying to tear my
clothes off . . .

LEONE [*to* GUIDO]: You see, Venanzi? In such a predicament
she actually managed to calmly think out matters and decide
that this was something that concerned me! That is such a
miracle that I am absolutely ready, here and now, to do
without further delay everything that can be expected of me!

GUIDO [*quickly*]: What? You'll do it?

SILIA [*stupefied, turning pale, hardly believing her ears*]: Do you
mean that?

LEONE [*softly and calmly, smiling*]: Of course I'll do it! Naturally! I'm sorry, but you're not logical!

GUIDO [*in a stupor*]: Who? Me?

LEONE: Yes, you, you! Don't you see that my doing it is the
exact and inevitable consequence of your discretion?

SILIA [*triumphant*]: You can't deny that's true!

GUIDO: How? [*Stunned.*] I don't understand. Why is it the
consequence of my discretion?

LEONE [*gravely*]: Just think a bit! If she was outraged like this,
and you were quite right to act discreetly, it obviously
follows that I must be the one to issue the challenge!

GUIDO: Not at all. Not at all. Because my discretion was due
to . . . because . . . because I realized that I should have had
to deal with four men who were so drunk that they didn't
know what they were doing!

SILIA: That's a lie!

GUIDO: Listen, Leone. They were drunk and they mistook
the door. And, anyway, they apologized.

SILIA: I didn't accept their apologies. It's easy to make excuses afterwards. I couldn't accept. But by the way Guido's talking anybody would think they had apologized to him! As though he was the one who'd been insulted! While all the time he kept himself well out of it, 'because he thought it would be more discreet'!

LEONE [*to* GUIDO]: There! Now you're spoiling everything, my dear fellow.

SILIA: It was *me* they insulted. Me!

LEONE [*to* GUIDO]: It was her. [*To* SILIA] And you immediately thought of your husband, didn't you. [*To* GUIDO] I'm sorry, Venanzi: it's obvious you don't think things out properly.

GUIDO [*exasperated, noting* SILIA'*s perfidy*]: Why should I think things out? I kept out of it last night, and you can leave me out of it now!

LEONE [*conceding the point and continuing in the same solemn tone*]: Yet you were right, you know, quite right to say that you would have compromised her. But not because they were drunk! That might, if anything, be an excuse for *me* – a reason why I shouldn't challenge them, and call upon them to make amends for their behaviour . . .

SILIA [*dismayed*]: What?

LEONE [*quickly*]: I said 'if anything', don't worry! [*To* GUIDO] But it can't possibly be an excuse for your discretion, because . . . well, if they were drunk you could perfectly well have been less 'discreet'.

SILIA: Of course he could! Men in their condition wouldn't have been shocked to find me entertaining a man in my flat. It wasn't yet midnight, after all!

GUIDO [*roused*]: Good Lord, Silia. Now you have the impertinence to suggest I ought to have done what you prevented –!

LEONE [*precipitately*]: No, no, no, no! He acted quite rightly – you said so yourself, Silia. Just as *you* were right to think of me! You both acted perfectly correctly.

GUIDO [*between two fires*]: No, I don't think . . . I . . . I don't know . . .

LEONE: Let me go on. I am delighted that, for the first time in her life, she has found an anchor – the one that keeps me tied to my allotted role of husband. Naturally, I don't want to break it for her. Yes, dear, yes! I'm 'The Husband', and you are 'The Wife', and he . . . why, of course! He's going to be 'The Second'!

GUIDO [*exploding*]: Oh no, I'm not! You can get that idea out of your head!

LEONE: Why not, pray?

GUIDO: Because I flatly refuse!

LEONE: You do?

GUIDO: Yes.

LEONE: But you are bound to accept. You can't help yourself.

GUIDO: I tell you I won't do it.

SILIA [*bitingly*]: Another sample of his 'discretion'!

GUIDO [*exasperated*]: Silia!!!

LEONE [*conciliating*]: Come now, please! Let us discuss the matter calmly. [*To* GUIDO] Now, Venanzi, do you deny that everybody calls upon your services in affairs of honour? Not a month passes without your having a duel on your hands. Why, you're a professional second! Come now, it would be ridiculous. What would people say – those that know you're such a close friend of mine and so experienced in these matters – if I, of all people, should turn to someone else?

GUIDO: Well, you certainly can turn to someone else, because I'm not going to do it.

LEONE [*looking him firmly in the eyes*]: In that case you ought to tell me your reason for refusing. And you can't! [*Changing his tone.*] I mean – you can't have a reason that will satisfy me – or anybody else.

GUIDO: It seems to me that I have a perfectly good reason. I think there's absolutely no occasion for a duel at all.

LEONE: That's not for you to say!

SILIA: I forced that man to leave me his card, and I showed it to everybody . . .

LEONE: Oh? Did someone else come in?

SILIA: Yes – they heard me shouting for help. And they all said it would be a good thing to give the Marquis a severe lesson.

LEONE [*To* GUIDO]: There! You see? A public scandal! [*To* SILIA] You're right! [*To* GUIDO] Come, come: it's no use arguing, my dear chap!

GUIDO [*giving up the position he has been maintaining in the hope of getting on the right side of* SILIA *once more*]: Oh, all right, then! I'll cart you off to the slaughter, if you like!

SILIA [*beginning to think better of it, since she finds herself left alone*]: Oh, Guido! Don't exaggerate now!

GUIDO: To the slaughter, Silia, to the slaughter! He will have it, so I shall take him off to the slaughter.

LEONE: No . . . really, you know, my wishes don't come into it. You're the one who *will* have it.

SILIA: But it isn't necessary to fight a duel to the death.

GUIDO: That's where you are wrong, Silia. There are only two alternatives: either to fight or not to fight. If there is a duel, it has to be fought in deadly earnest.

LEONE: Of course, of course!

SILIA: Why?

GUIDO: Because the mere fact of my going to demand a meeting would show that we don't consider they were drunk –

LEONE: – quite right –

GUIDO: – and the insult they did to you becomes doubly serious.

LEONE: Exactly.

SILIA: But it's up to you to suggest the terms – and you can make them easier.

GUIDO: How can I?

LEONE: Quite right. [*To* SILIA] He can't.

GUIDO: Moreover, if Miglioriti finds we are making no allowance for the state he was in, or for his apologies for his mistake, –

LEONE: – yes, yes! –

GUIDO: – he'll be so angry, –

LEONE: – naturally enough! –

GUIDO: – that he'll insist on the severest possible terms!

LEONE: It will seem a great provocation to him – a swordsman!

GUIDO: One of our best swordsmen, as I told you. Consider that point very carefully! And you don't even know what a sword looks like!

LEONE: No, that's true. But that's your worry. You don't expect me to concern myself with details like that, do you?

GUIDO: What do you mean, my worry?

LEONE: Because I'm certainly not going to worry about it.

GUIDO: You mean – it's my responsibility . . . to . . .

LEONE: It's all yours! And a very serious one. I feel sorry for you. But you must play your part, just as I am playing mine. It's all in the game. Even Silia has grasped that! Each of us must play his part through to the end. And you may rest assured that I shan't budge from my anchorage, come what may! I'm watching myself play my role and you two playing yours – and I find it all vastly entertaining.

[*The doorbell rings again.* PHILIP *enters from the Left. He crosses the stage in a furious temper and exits to the Right.*]

All that interests me is to get the whole thing over quickly. You go ahead and arrange everything . . . Oh, by the way, do you need any money?

GUIDO: Money now? Good Lord, no! Why?

LEONE: I've been told these affairs are expensive.

GUIDO: Well, we'll go into that later. Not now.

LEONE: Very well, we'll settle up afterwards.

GUIDO: Will Barelli suit you as a witness?

LEONE: Oh, yes . . . Barelli . . . or anyone else.

[PHILIP *re-enters with* DR SPIGA.]

Ah – Doctor Spiga. Come in, come in! [*To* GUIDO, *who has approached* SILIA *and is pale and agitated*] Look, Venanzi, we've even got the Doctor here. How convenient!

GUIDO: Good morning, Doctor.

LEONE: If you have confidence in him . . .

GUIDO: But really . . .

LEONE: He's a good chap, you know. First-rate surgeon. But I don't want to put him to too much trouble, so I'm wondering –

[*Turning to* GUIDO *who is talking to* SILIA.]

I say, do listen! You've left us standing here like a couple of hermits in the wilderness! I was going to say, the orchard is conveniently near, we could do it there, early tomorrow morning.

GUIDO: Yes, all right, leave it to me, leave it to me! Don't interfere! [*He bows to* SILIA.] Good-bye, Doctor. [*To* LEONE] I'll be back soon. No, wait, though! I shall have a lot to do. I'll send Barelli to you. I'll see you this evening. Good-bye.

[*He goes out to the Right.*]

SPIGA: What's all this about?

PHILIP: I say, don't you think it's about time . . .

LEONE: One moment, Socrates. Come over here, Spiga. First, let me introduce you to my wife . . .

SPIGA [*puzzled*]: Oh, but . . .

LEONE [*to* SILIA]: Doctor Spiga, my friend, fellow-tenant, and intrepid opponent in philosophical arguments!

SPIGA: Charmed, Signora. [*To* LEONE] So, you two have . . . ['*made up' understood*] . . . Well, I congratulate you, though, no doubt, to me it will mean the loss of a valued companionship to which I had become accustomed.

LEONE: Oh, no! What are you thinking?

SPIGA: That you've made it up with your wife.

LEONE: Oh, no, my dear fellow! We've never separated. We

live in perfect harmony – apart! There's no necessity for a reconciliation.

SPIGA: Oh . . . well, in that case, I beg your pardon. I . . . I must confess I couldn't see what my being a surgeon had to do with a reconciliation.

[*At this point* PHILIP *comes forward, unable to contain any longer his furious indignation against his master.*]

PHILIP: It has a lot to do with it, Doctor. And your surgery is only one of the absurd, mad things that go on here!

LEONE: Really, Philip, I . . .

PHILIP: Oh, I'm off, I'm off! I'm leaving you right here and now!

[*He exits to the kitchen, slamming the door.*]

LEONE: Spiga – go with him and try to calm him, will you? Bergson, my dear fellow, Bergson! Disastrous effect!

[SPIGA *laughs, then, pushed by* LEONE *towards the door on the Left, turns to bow to* SILIA. – *Then looks at* LEONE.]

SPIGA: But I still don't see how my surgery comes into it!

LEONE: Go on, go on! He'll explain it to you!

SPIGA: Hm! [*He exits.*]

[LEONE *goes to* SILIA *and stands behind the low chair in which she is sitting, absorbed. He leans over and looks down at her.*]

LEONE [*gently*]: Well, Silia? Have you something else to say to me?

SILIA [*speaking with difficulty*]: I never . . . never imagined . . . that you –

LEONE: That I?

SILIA: – would say 'yes'.

LEONE: You know very well that I have always said 'yes' to you.

[SILIA *jumps to her feet, a prey to the most disordered feelings: of irritation with this maddening placid docility on the part of her husband: of remorse for what she has done: of disdain for the lover who has first tried to get out of all responsibility, and*

*then, thinking to back her up, so as not to lose her, passed all
bounds.*]

SILIA: I can't stand it! I can't stand it! [*She is on the point of
weeping.*]

LEONE [*pretending not to understand*]: What? My having said
'yes'?

SILIA: Yes, that too! Everything . . . all this . . . [*alluding to*
GUIDO]. It will be your fault if it turns out to Guido's
advantage!

LEONE: My fault?

SILIA: Yes, yours! Through your insufferable, limitless
apathy!

LEONE: Do you mean apathy in general – or towards you?

SILIA: Your complete indifference, always! But especially
now!

LEONE: You think he has taken advantage of it?

SILIA: Didn't you see him just now? It seemed at first that
he wouldn't hear of a duel. Then finding you so accom-
modating, he went off to arrange . . . heaven knows what
terms!

LEONE: Aren't you being a little unfair to him?

SILIA: But I did tell him to try to make the terms easier, and
not to go too far now . . .

LEONE: But at first you egged him on.

SILIA: Because he denied everything!

LEONE: That's true. He did. But, you see, he thought your
attitude mistaken.

SILIA: And you? What do you think?

LEONE: Well, don't you see? I agreed to the duel.

SILIA: I suppose you think I exaggerated, too. Perhaps I did
a little – but I did it because of the way he was going on!

LEONE: Because he denied everything?

SILIA: But, because he denied everything, he surely could not
have found in my exaggeration any pretext for exaggerating
himself!

LEONE: Ah, but you irritated him, you know! You both exaggerated because you let emotion get the upper hand.

SILIA [*after a pause, looking at him in stupefaction*]: And you? Still unmoved?

LEONE: You must allow me to protect myself as best I can.

SILIA: Do you really think this indifference of yours can help you?

LEONE: Certainly! I know it can.

SILIA: But the Marquis is an expert swordsman!

LEONE: Let Signor Guido Venanzi worry about that! What does it matter to me what this fellow is?

SILIA: You don't even know how to hold a sword!

LEONE: It would be useless to me. This indifference will be weapon enough for me, be sure of that! There I have an inexhaustible source of courage – not merely to face one man, that's nothing – but to face the whole world, always. I live in a realm where no anxieties can trouble me, my dear. I don't have to worry about anything – not even death – or life! Just look at the ridiculous absurdity of men and their miserable, petty opinions! Don't you worry! I understand the game.

[*At this point, the voice of* PHILIP *is heard in the kitchen, saying*]

PHILIP: Well, go in your birthday suit, then!

[SPIGA *enters, Left.*]

SPIGA [*as he enters*]: In my birthday suit, indeed! Damned insolence! Oh . . . I beg your pardon, Signora. Leone, that manservant of yours is an absolute demon.

LEONE [*laughing*]: What's the matter?

SPIGA: What's all this I hear about a duel? Are you really involved in one?

LEONE: Do you find that difficult to believe?

SPIGA [*glancing at* SILIA, *embarrassed*]: Well . . . er . . . no! To tell you the truth, I really don't know what the devil that fellow has been telling me. You've actually sent the challenge, have you?

LEONE: Yes.

SPIGA: Because you considered –

LEONE – that I had to, of course. My wife has been insulted.

SPIGA [*to* SILIA]: Oh, I beg your pardon, Signora. I didn't realize. I . . . I . . . won't interfere. [*To* LEONE] As a matter of fact, you know, I . . . I've never been present at a duel!

LEONE: Neither have I. So that makes two of us. It will be a new experience for you.

SPIGA: Yes, but . . . I mean . . . what about the formalities? How should I dress, for example?

LEONE [*laughing*]: Oh, now I understand! That's what you were asking Socrates?

SPIGA: He told me to go naked. I shouldn't like to cut a poor figure.

LEONE: My poor friend, I don't know, either, what doctors should wear at duels. We'll ask Venanzi. He'll know.

SPIGA: And – I must bring my surgical instruments, I suppose?

[PHILIP *re-enters from the Left.*]

LEONE: Certainly you must.

SPIGA: It's on . . . serious terms, Philip tells me.

LEONE: So it seems.

SPIGA: Swords?

LEONE: I believe so.

SPIGA: If I bring my little bag . . . that'll be enough, eh?

LEONE: Listen – it's going to take place only a stone's throw away – in the orchard – so you can easily bring anything you feel you may need.

[*The doorbell rings.* PHILIP *exits to the Right.*]

SILIA: Surely that can't be Guido back so soon?

SPIGA: Venanzi? Oh, good. Then I can get him to tell me what I should wear.

[*Re-enter* PHILIP, *Right. He crosses the stage towards the door on the Left.*]

LEONE: Who was it?

PHILIP [*loudly, drily, and with an ill grace*]: I don't know. Some
gentleman or other with a sword.

[PHILIP *exits to the kitchen.* BARELLI *enters, Right, with two
swords in a green baize cover under his arm, and a case
containing a pair of pistols.*]

BARELLI: Good morning.

LEONE [*going to meet* BARELLI]: Come in, come in, Barelli.
What's all this arsenal for?

BARELLI [*indignantly puffing*]: Oh, I say, you know, look here,
my dear Leone: this is absolute madness! Sheer raving
lunacy!

[*Seeing* LEONE *pointing to* SILIA.]
Eh? What? What's that?

LEONE: May I introduce you to my wife? [*To* SILIA] This is
Barelli – a formidable marksman!

BARELLI [*bowing*]: Signora.

LEONE [*to* BARELLI]: Doctor Spiga.

BARELLI: How do you do?

SPIGA: Delighted. [*He shakes* BARELLI'S *hand, then, without
releasing it, turns to* LEONE] May I ask him?

LEONE: Not now. Later.

BARELLI: I've never heard of such a preposterous business in
all my life. [*To* SILIA] You must excuse me, Signora, but
if I didn't say so I should be neglecting my plain duty. [*To*
LEONE] You don't mean to tell me you've actually sent an
unconditional challenge?!

LEONE: What does that mean?

BARELLI: What!!! You've issued one without even knowing
what it is?

LEONE: How on earth should I know anything about such
matters!

SILIA: Please – what is an unconditional challenge?

BARELLI: One that can't be discussed: it gives us no chance
to try and settle the difference without fighting. It's against
all the rules and quite illegal – prohibited under the severest

60

penalties. And there are those two maniacs with the terms fixed up already – almost before they've set eyes on each other. By the way they were carrying on, it's a wonder they haven't decided on bombs and cannon as well.

SPIGA: Cannon?

SILIA: What do you mean?

BARELLI: Oh, the whole thing's crazy enough for that! First an exchange with pistols.

SILIA: Pistols?

LEONE [to SILIA]: Perhaps he's arranged that to avoid swords, you know. I expect Miglioriti is not so clever with a pistol.

BARELLI: Who, Miglioriti? Why, that fellow shoots the pip off the ace of spades at twenty paces!

SILIA: Was it Venanzi who suggested pistols?

BARELLI: Yes, Venanzi. What's the matter with him? Has he gone mad?

SILIA: Oh, my God!

SPIGA: But . . . excuse me, I don't follow. Where does the ace of spades come in?

BARELLI: What ace of spades?

LEONE: Quiet, quiet, Spiga. You and I don't understand these things.

BARELLI: First there's to be an exchange of two shots with pistols. Then you fall to with swords – and on what terms!

SILIA: Swords as well? Pistols weren't enough for him!

BARELLI: No, Signora – swords were chosen by agreement. Pistols were thrown in as an extra – out of bravado, as it were.

SILIA: But this is murder!

BARELLI: Yes, Signora. That's just what it is. But – if I may say so – it's up to you to stop it.

SILIA: Up to me? No! He's the one who can say the word! My husband. I never wanted it to become such a serious business.

LEONE [loudly and imperiously to BARELLI]: That's enough,

61

Barelli. I don't think there's much use your starting a discussion with my wife now.

BARELLI: No, but all the same ... there's something you don't know. The whole town is full of this affair. They're talking about nothing else.

LEONE: Already? How quickly tongues wag!

SILIA: And I suppose they all say that *I* am to blame.

BARELLI: No, no. Not you. Venanzi, Signora – Venanzi! You understand, Leone, nothing is being said against you – you don't come into it at all, in fact. Miglioriti's hatred and anger are directed against Venanzi alone, because he's found out – (and this is something that your own wife can confirm) – that Venanzi was there, in the flat, all the time. And he did nothing to stop them! Perhaps he was held back by – not exactly a grudge he had against Miglioriti – jealousy, rather, fencing-school jealousy. Heavens above! Venanzi keeps himself hidden out of the way ... he makes no attempt to stop them and prevent an ugly scandal (for they were only drunk, you know) – and on top of all that, now he turns up at Miglioriti's as the bearer of a challenge! The whole thing's incredible! Personally, I ... I don't know whether I'm on my head or my feet.

SPIGA: Listen, Leone, perhaps I could do something ...

LEONE [*in a sudden outburst*]: Don't attempt to interfere with things you don't understand my friend!

SPIGA: But, surely ... since it is to take place so near here ...

BARELLI: Yes, in the orchard – at seven tomorrow morning. Look, I have brought two swords.

LEONE [*quickly, pretending not to understand*]: Have I to pay you for them?

BARELLI: Pay? Good Lord, no! They're mine. I want to give you a little elementary instruction, and let you get the feel of it.

LEONE [*calmly*]: You want *me* to practise?

BARELLI: Of course! Who else? Me?

LEONE [*laughing*]: No, no, no, no, thank you. It's quite unnecessary.

BARELLI: How can you say it's unnecessary? [*He takes out one of the swords.*] I bet you've never seen a sword, to say nothing of the proper way of holding it.

SILIA [*trembling at the sight of the sword*]: Please! Please!

LEONE [*loudly*]: That will do, Barelli! Let's have no more of these jokes.

BARELLI: This is no joking matter! You must at least learn how to hold it . . .

LEONE: That will do, I tell you. [*Decisively.*] Listen all of you. I don't want to appear rude, but I'd like to be left alone now.

BARELLI: Oh, yes, of course, you must conserve your nervous energy. It's most important that you should keep calm.

LEONE: Oh, I shall keep calm, all right: you need have no doubts about that! But all this has been going on too long now: I need a breathing space, you see. If you want to play with those gadgets this evening when Venanzi comes, you two who are so brave can amuse yourselves with them for a bit while I watch. Will that do? Meanwhile, leave them here, and – and don't be annoyed if I ask you to go now.

BARELLI: Oh, very well. Just as you like.

LEONE: You too, Doctor, if you don't mind.

SPIGA: But won't you let me – ?

LEONE [*interrupting*]: You'll be able to ask Barelli for all the information you want.

BARELLI [*bowing to* SILIA]: Good-bye, Signora.

    [SILIA *barely inclines her head.*]

SPIGA: Good-bye, dear lady. [*He shakes her hand – to* LEONE] So long then, eh? Calm, you understand . . . calm . . . !

LEONE: Yes, all right. Good-bye.

BARELLI: Till this evening, then.

LEONE: Good-bye.

    [BARELLI *and* SPIGA *exeunt.*]

LEONE: Thank heaven they've gone. I really couldn't stand any more.

SILIA: I'll go too.

LEONE: No, you stay if you like – provided you don't speak to me about this business.

SILIA: That wouldn't be possible. And then – you'd never be sure of me, if Guido turned up here, as he may at any moment.

[LEONE *laughs loud and long*.]

SILIA [*wildly irritated at his laughter*]: Don't laugh. Don't laugh!

LEONE: I'm laughing because I'm genuinely amused, you know. You can't imagine how much I am enjoying watching you chop and change like this.

SILIA [*on the point of weeping*]: But doesn't it seem natural to you?

LEONE: Yes, and that's just why I'm enjoying it: because you're so natural!

SILIA [*promptly, furiously*]: But *you* are not!

LEONE: Isn't that a good thing?

SILIA: I don't understand you! I don't understand you! I don't understand you! [*She says this, first with almost wild anguish, then with wonder, then in an almost supplicating tone.*]

LEONE [*gently, approaching*]: You can't, my dear! But it's better so, believe me. [*Pause – then in a low voice*] I understand!

SILIA [*scarcely raising her eyes to look at him, terrified*]: What do you understand?

LEONE [*calmly*]: What it is you want.

SILIA [*as before*]: What do I want?

LEONE: You know – and yet you don't know what you want.

SILIA [*as before: as though putting forward an excuse*]: Oh, God, Leone! I think I must be going mad!

LEONE: Mad? Oh, no!

SILIA: Yes. I must have been mad last night. I'm terrified.

LEONE: Don't be afraid! I'm here.

SILIA: But what are you going to do?

LEONE: What I have always intended to do ever since you made me see it was my duty.

SILIA: I? Made you see your duty?

LEONE: Yes, *you* did.

SILIA: But, what is it?

LEONE [*softly, after a pause*]: To kill you! Do you think you haven't given me the motive to do it, more than once? Yes, of course you have! But it was a motive that sprang from a feeling, first of love – then of hate. I had to disarm those two feelings – to empty myself of them. And because I *have* emptied myself of them, now I can let the motive drop, and permit you to live – not as you want to live: you don't know that yourself: but as you *can* live, and are bound to, seeing that is impossible for you to do as I do.

SILIA: What do you do?

LEONE [*with a vague sad gesture, after a pause*]: I set myself apart. [*Pause.*] Do you imagine that impulses and feelings don't arise in me too? They do, indeed they do. But I don't let them loose. I bind them, and tame them. I nail them up. They're like wild beasts in a cage at a fair – and I am the tamer. Yet I laugh at myself sometimes as I watch myself playing this self-imposed role of tamer of my feelings. And then sometimes, I confess, a desire comes upon me to let myself be mangled by one of those wild beasts – yes, by you, too, looking at me now so meekly, so contritely. No, no! It's all a game, believe me. And that would be the last trick, that would take away for ever the pleasure of all the rest. No, no!

SILIA [*hesitant, as though offering herself*]: Do you want me to stay? [*She is trembling.*]

LEONE: Why?

SILIA: Or shall I come back tonight, when all the others have gone?

LEONE: Oh . . . no, dear. I shall need all my strength then . . .

SILIA: I mean, to be near you . . . to help you . . .

LEONE: I shall sleep, dear. Be sure I shall sleep . . . as I always do, you know, without dreams.

SILIA [*with profound grief*]: That's why everything's hopeless, you see! You won't believe it, but in bed my real love is sleep – sleep that quickly brings me dreams!

LEONE: Dreams, dreams! Oh, yes, I believe you. I believe you.

SILIA: But it never happens now. I can't sleep. And imagine what it will be like tonight! [*She breaks off.*] Well – I shall be here in the morning.

LEONE: Oh, no, no! You mustn't come. I don't want you to do that.

SILIA: You're joking!

LEONE: No, I mean it. I forbid you to come here tomorrow morning.

SILIA: You can't stop me. I shall certainly be here.

LEONE: Very well. Do as you please.

[*At this point* PHILIP *enters, Left – with the lunch-tray.*]

PHILIP [*in a hollow, surly, imperious voice*]: Hey! Lunch is ready!

SILIA [*passionately*]: Till tomorrow morning, then.

LEONE [*submissively*]: Till tomorrow morning . . .

[SILIA *goes out.* LEONE *remains absorbed in thought for a while, then goes and sits down at the table.*]

ACT THREE

The same as Act Two.
   The time is early the next morning.

   [*When the curtain rises, the stage is empty and almost dark.
   The front door bell rings.*
   PHILIP *enters Left, and crosses the stage.*]

PHILIP: Who the devil can it be at this hour? This is a fine
   beginning!
      [*He goes out, Right. After a moment he re-enters with* DR
      SPIGA, *who is dressed in frock-coat and top-hat, and carries
      two large bags full of surgical instruments.*]

SPIGA: Good morning, Philip.

PHILIP: 'Morning, Doctor.

SPIGA [*surprised at not seeing* LEONE]: Oh! Don't tell me he's
   still asleep?

PHILIP: Yes, he's asleep. Don't talk so loudly.

SPIGA: Good God, he's still asleep and I haven't shut my eyes
   all night!

PHILIP: Worrying about him? [*He points to the door at the back.*]

SPIGA: Yes, and trying to think of everything.

PHILIP: What have you got there? [*He points to the two bags.*]

SPIGA: Everything, everything! [*He goes to the dining-table
   which* PHILIP *has already partly laid.*] Come on, come on! –
   take off this table-cloth.

PHILIP: What for?

SPIGA: I've got my own here. [*Takes a surgical sheet of white
   American cloth out of one of the bags.*]

PHILIP: What are you going to do with that?

SPIGA: I'm going to get everything laid out in readiness here.

PHILIP: Oh, no, you're not! You don't touch that table. I'm
   laying it for breakfast.

SPIGA: Breakfast? Lord, man! We've something more important to think about than breakfast!

PHILIP: You leave that table alone, I tell you!

SPIGA [*turning to the writing desk*]: Well, clear the desk then.

PHILIP: You must be joking. If the police find out about the duel, don't you know that these two tables can talk?

SPIGA [*testily*]: Oh, yes! I know all about that. Don't you start quoting *him* at me! Two symbols: writing-desk and dining-table; books and cooking utensils; the void and the counter-balance? But don't you know that in about half an hour from now all those nonsensical ideas of his may be snuffed out like a candle?

PHILIP: Huh! Well, I suppose you've ordered his coffin, haven't you? You look like an undertaker.

SPIGA [*louder*]: My God, what an unfeeling brute you are! They told me to dress like this. This is really the limit. Heaven alone knows what a night I've had . . .

PHILIP: Hush! Not so loud!

SPIGA [*softly*]: . . . and now I have to argue with you. Get a move on! Clear this other little table for me at any rate. [*He points to the third, smaller one.*] I haven't time to waste.

PHILIP: Oh, I don't mind your using *that* one. It won't take long. [*He removes a cigar-box and a vase of flowers.*] There you are – cleared!

SPIGA: At last.

[SPIGA *spreads his cloth on the table and begins to get out his instruments. At the same time* PHILIP *goes on laying the breakfast table, occasionally disappearing into the kitchen to fetch things. The conversation continues meantime.*]

SPIGA [*to himself, checking his instruments*]: Scalpels . . . bone saw . . . forceps . . . dissectors . . . compressors . . .

PHILIP: What do you want all the butcher's shop for?

SPIGA: What do I want it for! Don't you realize he's going to fight a duel? Suppose he gets shot in a leg or an arm – we may have to amputate.

PHILIP: Oh, I see. Why haven't you brought a wooden leg, then?

SPIGA: You never know what may happen with fire-arms: you have to be prepared for anything. Look, I've brought these other little gadgets for bullet extraction. Probe . . . mirror . . . electric torch . . . scissors . . . two types of extractor . . . look at this one! English model – a beauty, isn't it? Now, where did I put the needles? Let . . . me . . . see . . . Mm . . . [*He looks in one of the bags.*] Ah, here they are! I think that's everything. [*Looks at the clock.*] I say, it's twenty-five past six! The seconds will be here at any minute!

PHILIP: So what? It's got nothing to do with me!

SPIGA: I'm thinking of him – suppose he isn't awake yet!

PHILIP: It's no good trying to keep him to his timetable today!

SPIGA: He made the appointment for seven o'clock.

PHILIP: Then he'll have to see to waking himself up. He may be up already.

SPIGA: You might go and see.

PHILIP: You don't catch *me* going to see! I'm his clock on ordinary days, and I'm not putting myself a minute fast or slow, today or any other day! Reveille, seven-thirty! –

SPIGA: Good God, man! Don't you realize that at seven-thirty today he may be dead?

PHILIP: – And at eight I bring him his breakfast!

[*There is a ring at the front-door bell.*]

SPIGA: There! You see? That'll be the seconds.

[PHILIP *goes out. He comes back shortly after with* GUIDO *and* BARELLI.]

GUIDO [*as he enters*]: Oh, good morning, Doctor.

BARELLI [*ditto*]: Good morning, Doctor.

SPIGA: Good morning. Good morning.

GUIDO: Are we all ready?

SPIGA: *I* am, quite ready!

BARELLI [*laughing at the sight of all the surgical armoury laid out on the table*]: Oh, look. Look, Venanzi, he certainly *has* got everything ready!

GUIDO [*irritated*]: Well, good God, there's nothing to laugh at! [*To* SPIGA] Has he seen it?

SPIGA: Who? Excuse me ... 'Quod abundat non vitiat.'

GUIDO: I'm asking you whether Leone has seen these instruments? [*To* BARELLI] You know, he must be absolutely calm but if he sees ...

SPIGA: Oh, no, he hasn't seen anything yet!

GUIDO: Where is he?

SPIGA: Well ... I think he's not up yet.

BARELLI: What?

GUIDO: Not up yet?

SPIGA: I *think*, I said: I don't *know*. He hasn't been in here.

GUIDO: Well, we can't stand about here like this. We have only a quarter of an hour left. He must be up. [*To* PHILIP] Go and tell him we are here.

BARELLI: What a man!

GUIDO [*to* PHILIP, *who has remained motionless, frowning*]: Get a move on!

PHILIP: At seven-thirty!

GUIDO: Oh, go to blazes! I'll call him myself. [*He rushes to the door at the back.*]

SPIGA: He's bound to be up ...

BARELLI: He really is amazing, upon my word!

GUIDO [*knocking loudly on the door, Centre, and listening, with his ear to it*]: What can he be doing? Surely he isn't still asleep? [*He knocks again, louder, and calls*] Leone! Leone! [*He listens.*] He is still asleep! My God, he's still asleep! [*He knocks again and tries to open the door.*] Leone? Leone!

BARELLI: What did I tell you? He's amazing! Incredible!

GUIDO: How does he lock himself in?

PHILIP: With the bolt.

GUIDO: But why?

PHILIP: I don't know.

BARELLI: Does he always sleep as soundly as this?

PHILIP: Like a log! Two minutes, it takes me to wake him, every morning.

GUIDO: Well, I'll wake him if I have to smash the door in! Leone! Leone! Ah, he's awake at last! [*Speaking through the door.*] Get dressed quickly. Hurry up. Hurry up. It's almost seven already.

BARELLI: Would you believe it!

SPIGA: What a sound sleeper!

PHILIP: Yes, he's always the same. He has to drag himself out of his sleep, as if he was hauling himself up from the bottom of a well!

GUIDO: Oh, is there any danger of his falling back again? [*He turns back to look at* LEONE'S *door.*]

BARELLI [*hearing a noise*]: No, listen: he's opening the door.

SPIGA [*placing himself in front of the table with his instruments*]: I'll keep him away from here!

[LEONE *appears, perfectly placid and still rather sleepy, in pyjamas and slippers.*]

LEONE: Good morning.

GUIDO: What! Still in pyjamas? Good Lord! Go and get dressed at once. You haven't a minute to lose, you know.

LEONE: Why, may I ask?

GUIDO: He asks why!

BARELLI: Have you forgotten you've a duel to fight?

LEONE: I? Fight a duel?

SPIGA: He's still asleep!

GUIDO: The duel, man! The duel! At seven o'clock!

BARELLI: In less than ten minutes.

LEONE: Don't get excited, I heard.

GUIDO [*absolutely dumbfounded*]: Well then?

LEONE: Well then what?

BARELLI [*also dumbfounded*]: What do you mean 'what'?! You've got to get dressed and go and fight!

LEONE [*placidly*]: Have I?

SPIGA [*as though to himself*]: He must have gone out of his mind!

LEONE: No, Doctor! I'm perfectly 'compos mentis'.

GUIDO: You have to fight.

LEONE: I have to fight, too, have I?

BARELLI: 'Too'? What do you mean?

LEONE: Oh, no, my friends. You're mistaken!

GUIDO: Do you want to withdraw?

BARELLI: Don't you want to fight, now?

LEONE: I? Withdraw? But you know perfectly well that I always firmly maintain my position.

GUIDO: I find you like this, and yet –

BARELLI: But, if you say –

LEONE: – How do you find me? What do I say? I say that you and my wife upset my whole day yesterday, Venanzi, trying to make me do what I admitted all the time was my duty.

GUIDO: Well then – !

BARELLI: – You're going to fight!

LEONE: That's not my duty.

BARELLI: Whose is it, then?

LEONE [*pointing to* GUIDO]: His!

BARELLI: Venanzi's?

LEONE: Yes, his.

[*He goes to* GUIDO *who has turned pale.*]

And you know it. [*To* BARELLI] He knows it! I, the husband, issued the challenge, because he couldn't for my wife's sake. But as for fighting the duel, oh no! As for fighting, [*to* GUIDO, *softly, pulling one of the lapels of his jacket, and stressing every word*] you know quite well, don't you, that that is no concern of mine, because I never fight against anybody – you're the one who fights!

[GUIDO, *in a cold sweat, passes his hand convulsively over his temples.*]

BARELLI: This is fantastic!

LEONE: No, perfectly normal, my dear fellow! Quite in

accordance with the rules of the game. I'm playing my part: he's playing his. I am not going to budge from my anchorage. And his opponent looks at it as I do, too. You said yourself, Barelli, that the Marquis is really angry with him, not with me. Because they all know, and you better than any of them, what he wanted to do to me. Yes, Venanzi, you and Silia really did want to cart me off to the slaughter, didn't you?

GUIDO [*protesting vigorously*]: No, I didn't! I didn't!

LEONE: Oh, yes, you and my wife were like two children bouncing up and down on a see-saw yesterday. And I was in the middle, balancing myself and you two into the bargain. You thought you'd have a little game with me, didn't you? You thought between you, you could win my life from me? Well, you've lost the game, my friends: I have outplayed you.

GUIDO: No! You are my witness that yesterday, right from the beginning, I tried –

LEONE: – Oh yes, you *tried* to be discreet. Very discreet!

GUIDO: What do you mean? What are you insinuating?

LEONE: Well, my dear fellow, you have certainly not been discreet up to the last, you must admit! At a certain point – for reasons I understand very well, mark you (and I'm sorry for you) – your discretion failed you. And now, I regret to say, you are about to suffer the consequences.

GUIDO: Because you're not going to fight?

LEONE: Exactly. It's not my business.

GUIDO: Very well, then. Is it mine?

BARELLI [*rising*]: 'Very well', do you say?!

GUIDO [*to* BARELLI]: Wait! [*To* LEONE] What are you going to do?

LEONE: I'm going to have breakfast.

BARELLI: But this is fantastic!

GUIDO: No, I mean . . . Don't you realize that if I take your place –

73

LEONE: – No, no, my dear Venanzi! Not mine: your own!

GUIDO: Very well, then: mine! But *you* will be dishonoured!

BARELLI: Disgraced! We shall be forced to expose your dishonour!

[LEONE *laughs loudly.*]

BARELLI: How can you laugh? You'll be dishonoured, dishonoured!

LEONE: I understand, my friends, and I can still laugh. Don't you see how and where I live? Why should I worry my head about honour?

GUIDO: Don't let's waste any more time. Let's go.

BARELLI: But are you really going to fight this duel?

GUIDO: Yes, I am. Don't you understand?

BARELLI: No, I don't!

LEONE: Yes, it really is his business, you know, Barelli!

BARELLI: You're being cynical!

LEONE: No, Barelli, I'm being rational! When one has emptied oneself of every passion, and . . .

GUIDO [*interrupting and gripping* BARELLI *by the arm*]: Come, Barelli. It's no use arguing now. Come down with me, too, Doctor.

SPIGA: I'm coming! I'm coming!

[*At this moment,* SILIA *enters, Right. There is a short silence during which she stands still, perplexed and amazed.*]

GUIDO [*coming forward, very pale, and grasping her hand*]: Goodbye, Silia. [*He turns to* LEONE] Good-bye.

[GUIDO *rushes out, Right, followed by* BARELLI *and* SPIGA.]

SILIA: Why did he say good-bye like that?

LEONE: I told you, dear, that it was quite useless for you to come here. But you were determined to.

SILIA: But . . . what are you doing here?

LEONE: Don't you know? I live here!

SILIA: And what is Guido doing? Isn't . . . isn't the duel going to take place?

LEONE: Oh, it will take place, I suppose. It may be taking place now!

SILIA: But . . . how can it be? If you're still here?

LEONE: Oh, yes, I am here. But he has gone. Didn't you see him?

SILIA: But then . . . that means . . . Oh, God! Why has he gone? Has he gone to fight for you?

LEONE: Not for me, dear – for you!

SILIA: For me? Oh, God! Did you do this?

LEONE [*coming up to her with the commanding, disdainful air of a cruel judge*]: Did I do this? You have the impertinence to suggest that I am responsible for it!

SILIA: But you have . . .

LEONE [*in a low voice, gripping her arm*]: I have punished you both!

SILIA [*as though biting him*]: I see! But at the price of your own dishonour!

LEONE: You are my dishonour.

SILIA: And all this time . . . God, what can be happening to him? It's horrible. Is he down there, fighting? Fighting on *those* terms! The terms he himself insisted on. [*She suddenly laughs hysterically.*] Oh, it's perfect! Perfect! And you let him have his way. I swear he never intended to fight, not he! You are the devil! The devil incarnate! Where are they fighting? Tell me? Down there? In the orchard? [*She looks for a window.*]

LEONE: It's no good, you know. There aren't any windows overlooking the orchard. You must either go down or climb up on to the roof.

[*At this point,* DR SPIGA, *pale as a corpse and all dishevelled, dashes in with grotesque discomposure: flings himself at his surgical instruments laid out on the table: rolls them up in the cloth, and rushes out without saying a word.*]

SILIA: Oh! Doctor! Tell me . . . tell me . . . what has happened? [*with a cry*] Oh! [*Not believing her own presentiments*]

Dead? [*Running out after him*] Tell me! Is he dead? Tell
me?

    [LEONE *remains motionless, absorbed in deep, serious thought.*
Long pause. PHILIP *enters, Left, with the breakfast tray and*
puts it down on the table.]

PHILIP [*calling in a hollow voice*]: Hey!

    [LEONE *barely turns his head.* PHILIP *indicates the breakfast*
with a vague gesture.]

Breakfast time!

    [LEONE, *as though he has not heard, does not move.*]

THE LIFE I GAVE YOU

La vita che ti diedi

TRANSLATED BY FREDERICK MAY

For permission to perform this play apply to the International Copyright Bureau, 26 Charing Cross Road, London WC2. For the right to use this translation apply to J. van Loewen Ltd., 81/83 Shaftesbury Avenue, London WI.

This play, translated by the late A. O. Roberts, was first presented in England at the Theatre Royal, Huddersfield, 11 May 1931, by the late Alfred Wareing, with the following cast:

DONN'ANNA LUNA	*Florence Kahn*
DONNA FIORINA SEGNI	*Amy McNeill*
LUCIA MAUBEL	*Dorothy Holmes-Gore*
FRANCESCA NORETTI	*Louise Regnis*
DON GIORGIO MEI	*G. Edward Hall*
LYDIA (LIDA)	*Norma Drayton*
FLAVIO	*Henry Cass*
ELISABETTA	*Mrs C. G. Archer*
GIOVANNI	*Cyril Grier*

Produced by Evan John

Frederick May's version of *The Life I Gave You* was first presented by the Pirandello Society at the Civic Theatre, Leeds, 10 September 1958, with the following cast:

DONN'ANNA LUNA	*Vicky Campbell*
DONNA FIORINA SEGNI	*Berthe Keightley*
LUCIA MAUBEL	*Audrey Priestley*
FRANCESCA NORETTI	*Mollie Campbell*
DON GIORGIO MEI	*Frederick May*
LIDA	*Jennifer Lorch*
FLAVIO	*Michael Beckham*
ELISABETTA	*Alwyn Hartley*
GIOVANNI	*Stanley Saville*

Produced by Frederick May

CHARACTERS

DONN'ANNA LUNA

LUCIA MAUBEL

FRANCESCA NORETTI, her mother

DONNA FIORINA SEGNI, sister to Donn'Anna

DON GIORGIO MEI, the parish priest

LIDA
FLAVIO } children of Donna Fiorina

ELISABETTA, the old nurse

GIOVANNI, the old gardener

TWO SERVANTS (women)

WOMEN OF THE NEIGHBOURHOOD

The scene is a lonely villa in the Tuscan countryside.
The time is the present (i.e. 1924).

ACT ONE

A cold room of grey stone – an almost naked room – in the lonely villa of DONN'ANNA LUNA. *A bench, a cupboard, a writing-table, and a few other pieces of antique furniture, which breathe a sense of peace exiled from the world. Even the light which enters the room through a spacious window seems to come from a life that is far far away. There is a door Back and another door in the wall Right; this second door is very much nearer to the door Back than to the proscenium arch.*

[*When the curtain rises a group of women from the neighbouring countryside is kneeling or standing before the door Right, which leads, one must suppose, into the room where* DONN' ANNA LUNA'S *son lies dying. The women, whether kneeling or standing, are bowed in an attitude of prayer, their hands clasped before their mouths. The ones who are kneeling are reciting in subdued tones the litany for those who are at the point of death, their foreheads almost touching the ground. The others keep looking anxiously and with dismay into the room Right, so that they shall observe the moment when death comes. At a certain moment they gesture to the first group to break off the litany, and, after a brief and anguished silence, they too kneel down and, one after another, chant the supreme invocations for the dead man.*]

THE FIRST GROUP [*they are on their knees; some of them speak the invocation, the remainder the prayer that follows*]:
Sancta Maria,

          Ora pro eo.
Sancta Virgo Virginum,

          Ora pro eo.
Mater Christi,

          Ora pro eo.

Mater Divinae Gratiae,

    Ora pro eo

Mater purissima,

    Ora pro eo.

THE SECOND GROUP [*they are standing; as the others reach this point, they gesture to them to cease chanting the litany; they remain poised for a moment, as if suspended in a gesture of anguish and dismay; then they too kneel down*].

ONE OF THEM: O Blessèd Saints of God, make haste to help him.

ANOTHER: Angels of the Lord, come and receive this soul.

A THIRD: O Jesus Christ, Thou Who hast called it unto Thee, receive his soul.

A FOURTH: And may the Blessèd Spirits guide his soul from Abraham's bosom into the presence of the Lord God Omnipotent.

THE FIRST: Lord, have mercy upon us.

THE SECOND: Christ, have mercy upon us.

A FIFTH: Grant him rest eternal, and make the eternal light of Thy Countenance to shine upon him.

ALL: May he rest in peace.

 [*They remain kneeling for a few moments longer, each of them reciting her own particular prayer in silence. Then they get up, crossing themselves as they rise. There enter, from the room in which the dead man is lying,* DONNA FIORINA SEGNI *and the parish priest,* DON GIORGIO MEI. *Clearly they are stunned and quite dismayed; their manner is instinct with compassion.* DONNA FIORINA, *a woman of about fifty years of age, is a moderately well-off provincial lady of the Tuscan countryside. She dresses according to the dictates of the latest fashion, as her children – who live in the big city – desire that she shall. (You know what children are like, don't you? The moment they begin to get the upper hand of their parents?) The clothes sit a little awkwardly on her old and bent body. There is, however, nothing outlandish about them.* DON

GIORGIO *is a fat and indolent country parish priest. He talks with difficulty, but this doesn't prevent him from always having to add something to what other people say, or to what he has himself said. Though there are times when he doesn't know exactly what to add. If, however, people give him time to speak after his own fashion and with due deliberation, he'll say things that are very wise and gracefully turned. For he is, when all's said and done, a lover of good reading, and no fool.]*

DON GIORGIO [*to the women, in a low voice*]: Go now, my daughters . . . Go now. And . . . And say another prayer . . . That God may look graciously on his blessèd soul.

[*The women curtsy, first to him, then to* DONNA FIORINA, *and go out through the door Back.* DONNA FIORINA *and* DON GIORGIO *remain silent for a long time.* DONNA FIORINA *is as if lost in dismay at the grief she is suffering on account of her sister, while* DON GIORGIO *is hovering between the disapprobation that he'd like to utter and the words of comfort that he doesn't know how to express. After a while* DONNA FIORINA *can no longer bear the picture that she has before her eyes – the picture of her sister's despair. She covers her face with her hands and throws herself down upon the bench.* DON GIORGIO *moves very quietly over towards her; he stands there for a moment or so, looking at her and shaking his head, and saying nothing; then he raises his hands in the gesture of one who remits the whole affair into the hands of God. And, please . . . I beg the actors not to be afraid of remaining silent, for silence speaks more eloquently than do words in certain moments . . . If the actors know how to make silence speak. And* DON GIORGIO *must remain standing by the figure of the woman huddled up on the bench for a little while yet. Then finally he is to say, his words coming like an appendix to his thoughts:*]

DON GIORGIO: And . . . And she's not so much as knelt down.

DONNA FIORINA [*sitting up on the bench, without uncovering her*

face]: If she goes on like this she'll go right out of her mind!
[*She takes her hands from over her face and turns to look at* DON
GIORGIO.] Did you see her eyes? ... And her *voice*! ...
When she ordered us to leave her alone?

DON GIORGIO: No. No. On the contrary, I should say myself
that reason is far too strongly developed in her, and ...
Well, I'm not so much afraid of her going out of her mind,
my dear Mrs Segni. No, I'm much more afraid lest she
should unhappily be deprived of the divine comfort of
faith, and that ...

DONNA FIORINA [*rising; she is fretful*]: But what is she doing
in there, all by herself?

DON GIORGIO [*trying to calm her*]: She's not by herself. She
was most anxious that Elisabetta should stay with her. So
don't worry yourself! Elisabetta's a good sensible soul,
and ...

DONNA FIORINA [*abruptly*]: Oh, if you'd only heard the way
she was talking last night! [*She breaks off when she sees the
old nurse,* ELISABETTA, *come out of the room in which the
body is lying.* ELISABETTA *walks in the direction of the door
Back.*] Elisabetta! [*And hardly has* ELISABETTA *turned round
before she is anxiously asking her – more with her gestures than
with her words*] What is she doing?

ELISABETTA [*her eyes are like those of a woman demented; her
voice is dull and toneless; she makes not a single gesture*]:
Nothing. She's looking at him.

DONNA FIORINA: Is she still not crying?

ELISABETTA: No. She's looking at him.

DONNA FIORINA [*in a frenzy*]: Oh, if she'd only cry! Oh,
God! If she'd only cry!

ELISABETTA [*first of all she comes over to them; then she stands
there, looking from one to the other; all the time she is like a
woman demented; in a low confiding voice she says*]: She keeps
on saying that he's ... There! [*She accompanies the word with
a gesture of the hand, as if to say, 'Far away'.*]

DON GIORGIO: Who? *He* is . . . ?

ELISABETTA [*nods*].

DON GIORGIO: *There? Where?*

ELISABETTA: She's talking to herself . . . Mutter. breath . . . Walking about the room . . .

DONNA FIORINA: And there's nothing we can do

ELISABETTA: And she's so sure she's right in wh ine's saying! It's terrifying just to be with her, listening to her!

DONNA FIORINA: But what else has she been saying? What else has she said?

ELISABETTA: She keeps saying, 'He's gone away. He'll come back.'

DONNA FIORINA: *He'll come back?*

ELISABETTA: Yes, that's what she says. She's absolutely sure.

DON GIORGIO: He's certainly gone away, all right. But, as for coming back . . .

ELISABETTA: Yes, she looked into my eyes and read that very thought there. So she repeated what she'd said, more loudly this time, and looking at me fixedly all the while: 'He'll come back! He'll come back!' Because, she says, the man who's stretched out in there before her eyes . . . She says it's not him.

DON GIORGIO [*in surprise*]: *That it's not him?*

DONNA FIORINA: That's exactly what she said last night!

ELISABETTA: And she wants him to be taken away at once.

DONNA FIORINA [*covers her face with her hands again*].

DON GIORGIO: To the church?

ELISABETTA: Taken away, is what she says. And she doesn't want him to be dressed.

DONNA FIORINA [*uncovering her face*]: And how does she want him to go, then?

ELISABETTA: The moment they told her he'd have to be dressed . . .

DON GIORGIO: Yes, of course. Before he got too stiff!

ELISABETTA: . . . When they told her, she shuddered with

...or. She's told me to get things ready for washing the body. Washed, wrapped in a sheet, and then away, out of the house. Just like that. I'll go and tell the women what they're to do and I'll be back immediately. [*And she goes out through the door Back.*]

DONNA FIORINA: Oh, she'll go out of her mind! She'll go out of her mind!

DON GIORGIO: Oh-Ha-H'm! We-ell! To tell the truth, the thought of putting clothes on a man who's stripped himself of everything . . . Maybe that's why she feels so reluctant to do it.

DONNA FIORINA: It may be . . . Perhaps. But I . . . I can't . . . I find it all so *confusing* . . . Yes! . . . Just trying to sort it all out.

DON GIORGIO: She wants to do things differently from everybody else.

DONNA FIORINA: Not because she just *wants* to! Oh, do believe that!

DON GIORGIO: I do believe it! But I can't help a little doubt creeping in. I can't help fearing that, by acting so differently from everyone else, so contrary to what is the usual practice . . . Well, I can't help fearing that she may lose her way and, her mind darkened, be without anyone with whom to share her sorrow, which is the sorrow of us all. Because, as you'll appreciate, another mother could quite well find utterly incomprehensible this desire of hers, that her son should be clothed only in the nakedness of death . . .

DONNA FIORINA: You're quite right! It's something I myself just can't understand!

DON GIORGIO: There, you see? And . . . And to pass from that to actually condemning her for . . . And . . .

DONNA FIORINA: She's always been like that! It seems as if she listens to what other people have to say to her . . . And then suddenly she bursts out . . . Just as if she were coming

86

back from a long way away ... With words that catch everyone unawares, so unexpected are they. She says things that are so very true, and when she says them it's just as if you could *touch* them. And then, a moment or so afterwards, when you come to think about them again, you find them absolutely staggering. Because they're the sort of thing that could never possibly enter anyone's mind. And you find yourself almost growing afraid at the thought of them. I'm really terrified, I swear I'm really terrified to hear her speak! I don't dare even to look at her. Oh, those eyes! Those eyes of hers!

DON GIORGIO: Ah, me! Poor afflicted mother!

DONNA FIORINA: To see her son disappear from life like that! In the short space of two days!

DON GIORGIO: Her only son. And he'd been back home again so short a time!

[*At this moment the old gardener,* GIOVANNI, *appears through the door Back, and takes a step or two in the direction of the door Right. His manner is one of utter dismay. He stands there for a moment, looking at the body in a stupor of anguish. He kneels down, and bows his head so low that it all but touches the ground. He remains like this for a few moments, while* DONNA FIORINA *and* DON GIORGIO *go on talking.*]

DONNA FIORINA: After having waited so many years for him to come back! So many years! It was more than seven years! He was a mere boy when he went away ...

DON GIORGIO: Yes, I remember. He went off to study engineering ... It was at Liége, if I remember correctly.

DONNA FIORINA [*she looks at him; then, shaking her head in disapproval, she says*]: Yes! Yes, Liége! And it was there that he later ...

DON GIORGIO [*with a sigh*]: Yes, I know! I know! And, as a matter of fact, I'm waiting here because I've got something to tell her about ...

[*He is alluding to the mother who is in the other room. The old gardener,* GIOVANNI, *gets up, crossing himself as he rises, and goes out through the door Back.*]

DONNA FIORINA [*waits until the old gardener is quite out of the room, and then immediately, anxiously, asks – alluding to the dead son*]: When he confessed to you, did he ask you to do something for him?

DON GIORGIO [*gravely*]: Yes.

DONNA FIORINA: Something to do with that woman?

DON GIORGIO [*gravely*]: Yes.

DONNA FIORINA: Oh, if only he'd married her when he first got to know her! When he was a student at Florence!

DON GIORGIO: She's French, isn't she?

DONNA FIORINA: Yes, she is *now*. But not by birth. No ... She's Italian. She was a student at Florence too. Then she married a Frenchman, a certain M. Maubel, who first of all carried her off to Liége ... Yes, precisely, Liége ... And then, later, to Nice.

DON GIORGIO: Ah, that explains things. And *he* followed her to Liége?

DONNA FIORINA: Oh, the suffering he caused his poor mother! Not to come back for seven whole years! He didn't even come back one single time to see her! Not even for a few days! And then, at last ... Yes, this is how it all had to end! To come back and die like this. In a matter of moments, as it were. And his relationship with that woman had not been broken off. No, it persisted still. But you'll know that already. He'll have confessed it to you. [*She looks at him and then says, hesitatingly*] Did he, perhaps, make arrangements for the children?

DON GIORGIO [*it is his turn to look at her*]: No. *Which* children?

DONNA FIORINA: Didn't you know that she had two children?

DON GIORGIO: Ah, you mean *her* children. Oh, yes! He *did*

tell me. And he told me that they had been their mother's salvation. And his too.

DONNA FIORINA: Their *salvation*, did he say?

DON GIORGIO: Yes.

DONNA FIORINA: Then they're not . . . They're not his?

DON GIORGIO [*at once*]: Oh, no, my dear Donna Fiorina! We cannot unfortunately call pure a love that is adulterous, even though that adultery be confined to the mind and to the heart. But it is quite certain that . . . At least, he told me that . . .

DONNA FIORINA: If that's what he told you when he was at the point of death, then may God forgive me for what I have thought. Many is the time that his mother has assured me that that was how things were. But I must confess that I found myself unable to believe that it could possibly be true. Their passion was so very great that I . . . Yes, I even suspected that those two children . . .

DON GIORGIO: No, no.

DONNA FIORINA [*tensed, listening; she motions* DON GIORGIO *to be silent*]: Oh, my God! Can you hear her? She's talking . . . She's talking to him! [*Quietly she goes up to the door Right and stands there listening for a moment or so.*]

DON GIORGIO: Leave her be. It's the effect of her grief. She's wandering in her mind.

DONNA FIORINA: No. It's merely that things . . . Well, we see things in a certain way, think about them in a certain way. And this misfortune . . . We have *our* way of seeing that too. But what about *her* way of seeing it? Who knows what *she* thinks about it!

DON GIORGIO: You really ought to get her to come away. For a little while at least. She mustn't stay here all on her own like this.

DONNA FIORINA: It's impossible! I wouldn't even try.

DON GIORGIO: Well, at least take her back with you to your villa! It's so near that . . .

DONNA FIORINA: If only she would come! But she's not moved out of this house for more than twenty years. Always thinking. Always thinking. And so, little by little, she's become like a stranger to everything and everybody.

DON GIORGIO: H'm, there's nothing worse than brooding on the thoughts that are bred of solitude. Nothing worse. They swirl into the soul like the poisonous vapours of some noxious swamp . . .

DONNA FIORINA: But solitude is already there, living within her spirit. You've only got to look into her eyes to realize that no other life can invade her from outside herself. Nothing can distract her from that life which is within her. She's shut herself up here, in this villa, where the silence . . . There, upstairs! . . . When you walk through the vast empty rooms . . . It's terrifying! It's terrifying! It seems as if . . . Oh, I don't know how to put it . . . It seems as if, up there, Time plunges into an abyss. And the noise of the leaves, when there's a wind! And when I think of her here, all on her own, I feel such anguish in my heart. Oh, I can't tell you how much it hurts me! I find myself imagining that the wind has come to carry off her soul. In the old days, however, when her son was far far away, I knew where the wind was carrying her soul. But *now* . . . Where will it carry it *now*? [*Then, seeing her sister appear in the doorway right*] Oh, God! Here she is!

[DONN'ANNA LUNA *is very white. She is like a person in a trance. There is a light in her eyes, and a quality of voice upon her lips, that are so very peculiar to herself, that they set her aside in an almost religious solitude, a being apart from the people and the things that surround her. Alone — and with a strange sensation of newness about her. And this aloneness and this strange newness of hers are all the more disturbing for being expressed with an almost divine simplicity. She speaks as if from a state of lucid delirium — a delirium that is (or so you might say) the tremulous breath of the inner fire that is*

THE LIFE I GAVE YOU

*devouring and consuming her in this terrible way. She walks
towards the door Back, without saying a word. She pauses
for a moment on the threshold and then catches sight of*
ELISABETTA, *now on her way back, accompanied by two
of the women servants who are carrying a large bowl of hot
water infused with balsam. Impatiently – but her impatience
is slight and instinct with grief –* DONN'ANNA *says*]

DONN'ANNA: Oh, do make haste! Do make haste,
Elisabetta! And do what I told you. But do be quick!
[*The two servants cross the stage, from one door to the other,
without stopping.*]

ELISABETTA [*apologetically*]: I had to tell them about the other
things you wanted doing . . .

DONN'ANNA [*in order to cut short her apologies*]: Yes! Yes!

ELISABETTA [*continuing nonetheless*]: . . . And then there'll be
the Doctor . . . He'll be coming up to see . . . And then
we'll have to allow some time for . . .

DONN'ANNA [*to cut things short*]: Yes! Yes! Now, off you go!
Off you go! Oh, look! Down there! [*And she points to the
floor near* ELISABETTA'S *foot.*] A rosary. One of the women
must have dropped it. [ELISABETTA *bends down and picks it
up. She hands it to* DONN'ANNA *and goes off towards the door
right. Just before* ELISABETTA *disappears through the door,*
DONN'ANNA *repeats her command.*] Exactly as I told you,
Elisabetta.

ELISABETTA: Yes, ma'am. Don't you worry. [*Exit.*]

DONN'ANNA [*looking at the humble rosary*]: To pray . . . To
set your grief down on its knees . . . Take it, Don Giorgio.
[*She hands him the rosary.*] It's more difficult for me. I must
stand and suffer. I must follow His will, from instant to
instant. Then there comes that moment when you almost
cease to breathe. Your courage fails you, and you pray,
'O, my God! I can't stand it any longer! Make my knees
bend beneath me!' He refuses. He wills that we shall *stand*
and suffer . . . He wants us erect and living. Living out our

lives here. Here! Instant by instant. With never a moment's rest.

DON GIORGIO: But, my dear lady, the true life is that which lies beyond the grave!

DONN'ANNA: I know that God cannot die in every one of His creatures that dies. And you cannot even tell me that my child, the creature of *my* body, is dead. You tell me instead that God has taken him back unto Himself.

DON GIORGIO: Yes, er, precisely!

DONN'ANNA [*in a voice that tears your heart*]: But, Don Giorgio, *I'm* still *here*, in *this* world!

DON GIORGIO [*at once, to try and comfort her*]: Yes! Oh, my poor, dear Donn'Anna!

DONNA FIORINA: Yes! My poor, dear Anna!

DONN'ANNA: And don't you feel that as far as we're concerned God isn't *there*, in that life beyond the grave, so long as He wants to go on living here in me and in us? Wants to go on living, not for our sake alone, but in order too that all those who have gone away may continue to live?

DON GIORGIO: May continue to live in our memories. Yes.

DONN'ANNA [*she looks at him as if the word 'memories' has wounded her. She turns her head very, very slowly – rather as if she didn't wish to see the wound. She goes and sits down. Then she says to herself, in a voice that is laden with grief, yet cold, cold . . .*]: I can't bear to talk any longer. Nor can I bear to hear anyone else talking.

DONNA FIORINA: Why not, Anna?

DONN'ANNA: It's the words. And the way I hear other people using them!

DON GIORGIO: I only said 'memories'.

DONN'ANNA: Yes, Don Giorgio. But the word was like a kind of death to *me*. I've never had any other life but this one . . . *His* life. *Have* I ever lived any other life but this? No, this is the only life that I can *touch*. Clear-cut and vividly present. You say the word 'memories' to me, and at once it begins to fade away into the distance. I feel it slipping away from me.

DON GIORGIO: And what should I say, then?

DONN'ANNA: You should tell me that God wants my son to continue to live for me! That's what you should tell me! Oh, not with the sort of life that it was His will that he should enjoy when he lived here among us. I realize that. No, with the sort of life that *I* have *always* given him! Yes, *always*! And this life can never die in him so long as life shall persist in me. And isn't it true that, if by our deeds we make ourselves worthy, we may live eternally? Yes, even here on earth! My son will not live eternally. No. But he shall live here with me. He shall live the life of this day, of which but half has been left to him. And he shall live the life of tomorrow. As long as I shall live my son shall live too. He *must* live! He must live here, with everything that belongs to this life ... Here on earth ... He must live clothed in the whole garment of my life ... That is *his* life! ... The life that belongs to him and that no one can take away from him!

DON GIORGIO [*with a compassionate gesture he recalls her from what he sees as too great a spiritual pride, in an endeavour to make her see reason. He raises his hand and points to God*].

DONN'ANNA [*at once, understanding his gesture*]: No. God? God doesn't take away life!

DON GIORGIO: I was speaking of the life that formerly was his, here on earth.

DONN'ANNA: Because you know that there's a poor corpse in there that can no longer see you or hear a word you say. And that's good enough for you, isn't it? It's all over and done with. Yes! Yes! Dress him up once again in one of the suits he brought back from France with him! Even if it's utterly useless as a protection against the cold that is now within him. The cold that no longer assails him from without.

DON GIORGIO: But, my dear Donn'Anna, it's only what's usually done . . .

DONN'ANNA: Yes! You recite prayers. You light candles. Yes! You're busy *doing*. Yes! But mind you do it quickly! I want his room in there to remain just as it was . . . I want it to be there . . . A room that is alive . . . A room that is alive with the life that I shall give it . . . Waiting for him to come back . . . Filled with all the things that he left in my care before he went away. But you know, don't you, that my son . . . The one who went away . . . *He* hasn't come back yet. [*She intercepts a glance that* DON GIORGIO *is sending in the direction of her sister.*] Don't look at Fiorina like that. And neither have *her* children! Flavio and Lida went away last year, and left her. Went away to live in town. Do you think they'll come back to her? [DONNA FIORINA, *hearing her talk like this, begins to weep quietly.*] No, don't cry! I cried too . . . *Then* . . . Oh, yes! . . . I cried for a long, long time. Because he'd gone away! Without knowing why! Just as you're crying without knowing why! You haven't the faintest idea why you're crying!

DONNA FIORINA: No! No! I'm crying because of you, Anna!

DONN'ANNA: And haven't you yet understood that that would mean that we should be for ever weeping? Oh, Fiorina! [*She takes her head between her hands, and looks lovingly into her eyes.*] Is this really you? Is this *your* sad brow? These *your* sad eyes? Do you ever think about yourself? How could you let yourself become so changed from what you were once upon a time? I see you still, just as you were then . . . All alive . . . Really and truly a little flower . . . Just like your name! Do you really want me not to have it seem a dream, seeing you now as you were then? Yes, it *is* a dream! And you . . . Tell me the truth . . . If you ever find yourself thinking about it, how does it seem to you – the picture of yourself as you were once upon a time?

DONNA FIORINA: You're quite right, it *is* just like a dream, Anna. Yes.

DONN'ANNA: There, you see? You see how things are? That's what everything's like ... A dream. And your body ... If it changes like this ... Takes on a different shape for you, even as your hand reaches out towards it ... And the images of yourself that result ... This one ... *That* one ... What *are* they, these pictures of yourself? The memories of dreams. There you are: the dream of today; yesterday's dream. Everything's a dream.

DONNA FIORINA: Yes, the memories of dreams.

DONN'ANNA: Well then, so long as the memory's alive, I say, that's all that's needed for the dream to become life! You see? My son, as *I* see him, is *alive*! *Alive*! I'm not talking about the body that's lying in that room there! Oh, do try to understand me!

DONNA FIORINA [*almost to herself*]: But it's still your son who's lying in there!

DON GIORGIO: Oh, would to God that it really were a dream!

DONN'ANNA [*her impatience quite gone; she pauses for a moment before she speaks, a moment of self-absorption*]: It takes seven years ... As I know only too well ... It takes seven years of doing nothing but thinking about the son who doesn't come back, seven years of suffering what I've suffered, in order to understand this truth ... This truth which is greater than any grief, and which is transmuted here, *here*, into a light that can never again be put out. [*She presses her hands to her temples.*] This truth which smites you with the terrible cold fever that dries up your eyes, dries up the very inflexion of your voice. A bright light, and a cruel one. I almost find myself turning round at the sound of my own voice ... Just as if someone else were speaking.

DONNA FIORINA: You must rest for a little while, my dear Anna!

DONN'ANNA: I can't rest. I must remain alive for *his* sake. But look, Don Giorgio . . . Don't you think it's true, all that I've just said? You believe that my son's dead now, don't you? But he's not dead for *me* now. You see, I wept all the tears I had to weep, secretly, when I saw him come back to me. And that's the reason why I now have no more tears to shed! I wept when I saw come back to me a stranger, a man in whom there was no longer to be discovered anything of my son.

DON GIORGIO: Ah, yes! Yes! That's it . . . He was *changed*! Yes! And you said the very same thing yourself just now, about your sister. But, you know, life changes us all, and . . .

DONN'ANNA: . . . And we think we can comfort one another by saying, 'Changed', just like that. 'Changed' – doesn't that mean that one's different from what one was? And if what *was* previously *is* no longer, what possible meaning can your word 'changed' be said to have? I could no longer recognize him as that son of mine who'd gone away. I kept looking at him, trying to find at least a hint of him: of the way he'd look at you; of the smile that used to hover so faintly, as if it were brushing his lips . . . Oh, I don't know! . . . Hoping to see again that sudden light which would appear upon his brow . . . Oh, how lovely it was! . . . The brow of a youth just emerging into manhood! And his lovely hair – so rich and so fine. It shone like gold in the sunlight! If only he could have recalled for me my living son! If only for a moment! If only he could have made me see in him, the man who had returned, my son as once upon a time he had been. No. No. These were the eyes of a stranger, cold eyes. And an eternal sombre dullness upon his brow, and that tightness here, at the temples. And all but bald. His hair almost all gone. Yes, looking just as he looks now, lying in there. [*She gestures in the direction of the room in which the body is lying.*] But you must admit that I know my son, my son as once he was. A mother looks at her son and she knows him, knows him just as he is. My God, wasn't it she who created him in her womb? Well, life can behave so very cruelly towards a mother. It tears her son away from her and . . . *Changes* him! A stranger. And I didn't know anything about it. He was dead, and I went on making him live in me.

DON GIORGIO: But it was for *you*, my dear Donn'Anna, that he was dead. That was how he seemed to *you*. He wasn't dead for himself, since he went on living until just a short while ago . . .

DONN'ANNA: Yes, he went on living his life! Yes, he went on living his life! The life that he gave *us*, gave *me*. But it was very little of his life that he gave *me* when he came back, almost nothing of it, in fact. It was all given to *her*, every particle of it . . . Always! [*She gestures into the distance.*] Now do you understand what horrible things it has fallen to my lot to suffer? My son . . . My son, who continues to live on in my memory, remained there, there with that woman, there in her heart. And there returned to me that other man. And I couldn't even tell how it was that he saw me, so changed were his eyes. A man who could no longer give me anything. And even when, as sometimes he would, he'd touch me with his hand, I no longer felt anything of what I'd felt before. And what can I know of his life as it had then become for him? What can I possibly know of things as he saw them? And when he'd touch something, what could I possibly know about what he felt? You see . . . That's how things are. That is how things are. What we have lost is merely something that we don't know, something that we can't possibly know: life as he gave it to himself and to us. Yes, it is that life which we are mourning now. But if that's so, then, my God! we ought to be able to understand too that the real reason why we weep even in the presence of death is quite, quite different from the one for which we believe we're weeping!

DON GIORGIO: We weep for the one whom it has fallen to our lot to lose.

DONN'ANNA: There, you see? That life of ours which was the creation of the person who dies, the thing we know nothing about!

DON GIORGIO: Why no, Donn'Anna . . .

DONN'ANNA: Yes! Yes! It's for ourselves that we weep! Because the person who dies can no longer give . . . Oh, my son! My son! . . . Can no longer give even the slightest particle of life to us. No life can come to us from those eyes, eyes in which the light is quite extinguished, eyes that can no longer see us. No life can come to us from those hands of his, cold, hard hands, hands that can no longer touch us. And why should you want me to weep, then, if it is only for myself that I should weep? When he was far, far away, I used to say to myself, 'If at this moment he is thinking of me, then I am alive for him.' That thought sustained me, comforted me in my loneliness. What ought I to say now? I ought to tell myself that I, I am no longer alive for him, since he can no longer think of me! And yet you, on the other hand, are trying to tell me that *he* is no longer alive for *me*. But of course he's alive for me! He's alive, alive with all the life that I have always given him! *My* life! *Mine!* Not *his* life! For that is a life I cannot know! He lived it out, that life of his, far, far away from me, and I knew nothing whatsoever about it. And if for seven years I could give him my life, without his ever being near me, don't you think I can possibly go on giving him that life? Still go on giving him that life in the same way as before? What more of him is there that's dead that wasn't already dead as far as I was concerned? I've learnt to see very clearly that life doesn't depend for its existence upon whether or not there's a body upon which we may gaze. The body may be there indeed, there before our eyes, and yet it may still be dead as far as the life we gave it is concerned. Those eyes of his ... Sometimes they'd suddenly widen, as if a totally unexpected flood of cheerful light had come into them. They'd be suddenly filled with laughter and limpid happiness. Well, he'd lost those eyes in the life that he was living. But in that life of his which lived in me ... No, in that life they were *not* lost. In that life he has them still ... And will have them always ... Those eyes of his. If I call him he turns towards me! And his eyes suddenly laugh out at me, full of limpid happiness! He is *alive*! And this means that now I must never again let him go away from me, for it is in me that he has his life. I must never again allow any other life to come between him and me. Yes! *Yes!* My life here shall be dedicated to him. He shall live in the sight of my eyes, that shall see him, and in the words upon my lips, that shall speak to him. And it may even happen, perhaps, that I shall be able to make him live for her, in her heart, where he wished to live. And I shan't mind if he never again gives me anything of that life of his which dwells within her heart. I shan't mind if he gives me nothing of it, if he wishes not to. My whole life, in all its entirety, shall be his, his as he lives in her. He shall live my life, and I shall stay here in this house, waiting for him to come back. Waiting, just in case he should ever succeed in freeing himself from his desperate passion for her. [*Then, to* DON GIORGIO] You know all about it.

DON GIORGIO: Yes, he told me about it.

DONN'ANNA: I had presumed that he had, Don Giorgio.

DON GIORGIO: And he also told me how he wanted the news of his death broken to her.

DONN'ANNA [*just as if her son were speaking with her lips*]: For the love that he bore her failed in him never, not even in his final moment.

DON GIORGIO: Yes! He wanted us to take all proper precautions in the way we told her ... To write in the first place to her mother, who's staying with her.

DONN'ANNA [*again it is just as if her son were speaking with her lips*]: For this love of his shall never fail. He shall love her for evermore!

DON GIORGIO [*in utter bewilderment*]: What? How?

DONN'ANNA [*completely naturally*]: If she can come to know the way to keep him alive in her heart, by waiting for him to return from me to her there, just as I am waiting here for him to come back from her. If she loves him she will understand what I mean. It was their good fortune that their love was such that they had no need of the body's presence in order to live. That was how they loved one another. They can, then . . . Yes, they can go on loving one another still.

DONNA FIORINA [*in consternation*]: But what are you saying, Anna?

DONN'ANNA: I say that they can go on loving one another! In *her* heart! If she can find the way to give him, to go on giving him, *life*, the life of her love. The life that at this moment she is undoubtedly giving him – if she is thinking of him as here and alive, just as I am thinking of him as alive and with her.

DON GIORGIO: But, my dear Donn'Anna, do you really believe that one may by-pass death just like that?

DONN'ANNA: No, that's not what I mean! Not 'just like that'. That would be very wrong. Yes, life has always placed a stone upon the dead. So that it may pass on in fancy free. But it must be *our* life, not the life of the dead. Oh, we always want the dead to be well and truly dead, so that we can go on living our life in peace and quiet. And in that way it's a fine and handsome thing to by-pass death!

DON GIORGIO: Why, no! It's one thing to forget the dead – a thing we should never do, dear Donn'Anna – quite another to think of them as still alive, as you suggest . . .

DONNA FIORINA: Waiting for him to come back . . .

DON GIORGIO: . . . when you know that he can never again come back!

DONN'ANNA: So I must think of him as dead, must I? Dead . . . Just as he is . . . There in that room . . .

DON GIORGIO: Unfortunately! . . .

DONN'ANNA: And rest in the certainty that he can never again come back! I must weep! Weep till my heart breaks! And then, little by little, grow calmer, less troubled . . .

DONNA FIORINA: . . . find consolation of some sort!

DONN'ANNA: And then . . . From time to time . . . Remember him . . . As if he were something far away and long ago. 'This is what he was like.' 'This is the sort of person he was.' 'He said this.' Is that the sort of thing you want?

DONNA FIORINA: It's only what everyone else has always done, my dear Anna!

DONN'ANNA: You mean, in fact . . . Yes, you want me to *make* him die, to make him die even in us. Not suddenly become dead, in the way that the man who's lying in there is dead, but little by little . . . By forgetting him, by denying him the life that formerly we gave him. Just because now he can no longer himself give any life to us. Is that what one must do? So much . . . And for just so long. You no longer give me anything. All right, I shall no longer give you anything. Or, at most . . . Taking into consideration the fact that if you no longer give me anything it's because you *can't* give me anything any longer, because you haven't even a shred of life left to you, not the tiniest crumb! But look! I'll give you a scrap or two of what I've got left over. Every now and again I'll remember you . . . Just like that . . . Just as if you were something that happened far away and long ago. Ah, yes! We must be very careful about *that*! You must be very far away! Lost in the distance! So that you shall never by any chance be able to come back. For if you were to . . . Oh, my God! How terrible that

would be!... There! There you have the perfect death.
And there too you have the life that even a mother, if she
wishes to be a wise and sensible woman, must go on
living ... When for her her son is dead.

[*At this moment* GIOVANNI, *the old gardener, appears again
on the threshold of the door back. His manner is one of great
dismay, and he is carrying a letter in his hand. Catching sight
of* DONN'ANNA *he stops short and doesn't come into the
room. He signals to* DONNA FIORINA *about the letter, taking
great care not to be seen by* DONN'ANNA. *But she, seeing
her sister and* DON GIORGIO *turn in his direction, turns to
look at him too, and, perceiving his dismay, asks*]

DONN'ANNA: Giovanni!... What's the matter?

GIOVANNI [*hiding the letter*]: Nothing. I just wanted to ... I
just wanted to tell Donna Fiorina that ...

DON GIORGIO [*who has caught sight of the letter that the old man
has in his hand, asks anxiously, in some consternation*]: I wonder
if that's the letter he was waiting for.

DONN'ANNA [*to Giovanni*]: *Have* you got a letter there?

GIOVANNI [*hesitantly*]: Yes, but ...

DONN'ANNA: Give it to me. I know that it's for him. [*The
old man hands the letter to* DONN'ANNA *and exit.*]

DON GIORGIO: He was waiting for it so anxiously ...

DONN'ANNA: Yes, for the last two days! Did he speak to you
about it too?

DON GIORGIO: Yes. He told me that you were to open it
the moment it arrived.

DONN'ANNA: That *I* was to open it? *I* ... ?

DON GIORGIO: Yes. So that you could ... Should it happen
to be necessary ... Avert in time a risk that ... Oh, he
suffered terribly thinking about it ... Right up to the last
moment ...

DONN'ANNA: Oh, yes! I know! I know!

DON GIORGIO: He saw that there was the danger of her
committing the folly of ...

DONN'ANNA: ... of coming and joining him here! Oh, yes! I know! He fully expected her to come! He fully expected her to abandon her children, her husband, her mother!

DON GIORGIO: And so as to prevent this act of folly he told me that he had, as a matter of fact, already begun to write a letter ...

DONN'ANNA: ... to *her*?

DON GIORGIO: Yes.

DONN'ANNA: Well, in that case, it'll be over there! [*She gestures in the direction of the writing-table.*]

DON GIORGIO: Perhaps. If it is, we must destroy it now, so as to carry out his other suggestion, that we should write to her mother. But let's see, let's see, first of all, what it is she's written.

DONN'ANNA [*with trembling hands she opens the letter*]: Yes! Yes!

DON GIORGIO: I stayed behind on purpose to tell you about this. And now the letter's come.

DONN'ANNA [*taking the letter out of the envelope*]: Here it is! Here it is!

DONNA FIORINA: A letter to *him*! And he's no longer here!

DONN'ANNA: No, you're wrong! He *is* here! He *is* here! [*And she begins silently to read the letter. As she reads, the expressions that come upon her face, the trembling of her hands, and the exclamations that from time to time burst from out of her heart, all make manifest the joy that she feels at experiencing her son's being alive in the passion of his far-off mistress.*] Yes ... Yes ... She *does* say that she wants to come ... She's coming! She's coming!

DON GIORGIO: In that case we must prevent her ...

DONNA FIORINA: At once!

DONN'ANNA [*going on reading, without paying the slightest heed to what they're saying*]: She can't stand it any longer! So long as she had him there beside her ... [*Then, in a sudden outburst of tenderness*] Oh, how lovingly she writes to him!

How beautifully she writes to him! [*She goes on reading the letter, and then in an another outburst, in which laughter blends with the vehemence of her cry, she says, her voice, as it were, glistening with tears*] You *can?* You *can?* So you too can . . . Yes, you can! [*Then, her voice taking on the note of grief*] Ah! But she despairs of . . . ! [*Going on with her reading.*] This torment . . . Yes . . . [*For a moment she stops reading and ponders. She resumes her reading for a few more moments, and then exclaims*] Oh, such love! Yes, so much love! [*Then, shortly after, her expression changes*] Oh! Oh, no! No! [*Then, as if replying to the letter*] But he *is!* Yes, he *is!* It's true for him too! All the time that he's here! Yes, it's true for him as well! Yes, he's yours! Always yours! [*Then, in a transport of joy*] She can see him! She can see him! [*Then, suddenly becoming perturbed*] Oh, my God! It's driving her to despair! She's utterly desperate! . . . No! Oh, no! [*She breaks off her reading, and turns to* DON GIORGIO *and her sister.*] It's quite impossible! Quite, quite impossible! We can't choose this moment to tell her that he can never again give her the comfort of his love, the comfort of his life!

DON GIORGIO: That's the very reason why he himself suggested that . . .

DONNA FIORINA: . . . that we shouldn't tell her directly!

DON GIORGIO: Her mother will think of a way to . . .

DONN'ANNA: Impossible! She'd either die from grief or go out of her mind! No! No!

DONNA FIORINA: But, Anna, we must . . . Somehow we must . . .

DONN'ANNA: There's no must about it! If you could only hear how alive he is! How completely alive he is, here in this desperation of hers! If you could only hear how she speaks to him of her love! How she cries aloud her love for him! She threatens to kill herself! Oh, what a terrible disaster it would be for her, were he not so completely alive for her at this moment!

DONNA FIORINA: But, my dear Anna, how can he be? In what way can he possibly be . . . ?

DONN'ANNA: There's the letter that he began to her! Over there! [*She goes over to the writing-table and opens the writing-pad that's lying on it. From it she takes her son's letter.*] Here it is!

DON GIORGIO: And what do you intend to do with it, Donn'Anna?

DONN'ANNA: He'll have known how to find the right words to comfort her. And they'll be here – living words. Words that can restrain her, dissuade her from her desperate plan to come here!

DON GIORGIO: And do you mean to send her this letter?

DONN'ANNA: Yes! I shall send it to her!

DON GIORGIO: No, Donn'Anna!

DONNA FIORINA: Think of what you're doing, Anna!

DONN'ANNA: I tell you that she still has need of his life! Would you have me kill him for her at this moment, and kill *her too*?

DONNA FIORINA: But you'll write to her mother at the same time?

DONN'ANNA: I shall write to her mother too, and ask her to persuade her daughter to let him go on living for her! Oh, leave me alone! Leave me alone!

DON GIORGIO: But the letter's not even finished!

DONN'ANNA: *I* shall finish it! His handwriting was exactly like mine. He wrote just like me! . . . *I* shall finish it!

DONNA FIORINA: No, Anna!

DON GIORGIO: Don't do it, Donn'Anna!

DONN'ANNA: Leave me alone! I want to be by myself. He still has this hand with which to write to her! And he *shall* write to her! He *shall* write to her!

ACT TWO

[*The scene is the same as in the previous Act. It is towards evening a few days afterwards. On either side of the window in the wall Left there is a flower-pot containing a tall plant in full and vigorous flower. A third and similar pot is being carried in by* GIOVANNI *when the curtain rises. He is standing in the doorway Back, with the flower-pot in his hands. Near the door are* DONN'ANNA *and her sister,* DONNA FIORINA.]

DONN'ANNA [*to* GIOVANNI, *pointing to where she wants him to put the flower-pot – that's to say, just by the door, to the right*]: Here, Giovanni! Put it down here! [GIOVANNI *puts it down.*] That's it. Now go and get the last one, and put it on the other side, so that they balance one another. If it's too heavy for you, get someone to give you a hand.

GIOVANNI: No, it'll be all right, ma'am.

DONN'ANNA: Yes, I know! They couldn't be too heavy for you, could they? You're a good old man! Go on, then! Off you go! [*And as* GIOVANNI *is going out, she turns to her Right and says to* DONNA FIORINA, *as she sniffs the plant*] Smell, Fiorina! Isn't it a lovely smell? [*And then, pointing to the other plants by the window*] How lovely they are! *Here*, and *alive*!

DONNA FIORINA: But you're only making your task still more difficult by what you're doing! Have you thought of that?

DONN'ANNA: Folly for folly! Oh, leave me be, to do things as I... We never committed a single foolish deed, you and I, when we were young! Not of our own desiring, at any rate!

DONNA FIORINA: But it's you who're responsible for her folly... *Now!*

DONN'ANNA: No. He did his utmost, he tried in every possible way, to persuade her not to do it. She insisted on coming! Her heart was set on coming! Besides, there wouldn't have been time for me to prevent her from coming ... Not by writing! She's already left!

DONNA FIORINA: Oh, if you'd only written to her mother, before she ...

DONN'ANNA: I just couldn't! I tried ... Three days running I tried. But I couldn't do it. Because, you see, I'm still afraid.

DONNA FIORINA: Afraid of what?

DONN'ANNA: That things mightn't be the same for her as they are for me! And that when she 'got to know everything', her love must inevitably come to an end!

DONNA FIORINA: But that's what you *ought* to be wishing! That's what you *ought* to be wishing!

DONN'ANNA: You mustn't say that to me, Fiorina! She's written him another letter ... Did you know?

DONNA FIORINA: Another letter?

DONN'ANNA [*her eyes alight with a sombre voracious joy*]: I read it for him! [*And then, immediately – to forestall what her sister is going to say*] But it was much more bitter than the first one!

DONNA FIORINA: My God, Anna, you really terrify me!

DONN'ANNA: A mother, *terrified*! As if she had never carried her two children, living, within her womb! Never fed them, out of her living flesh! Never known that beautiful double hunger! Or *were* you terrified then? Now I am eating life for him! Suppose I were to call him ... What would you do? Would that terrify you too?

DONNA FIORINA [*she stops her ears, just as if her sister were in fact about to call out her son's name*]: No, Anna! Dear Anna, no! No!

DONN'ANNA: Are you afraid he might decide that it would be a good joke to come out of there ... Appear before you and punish you for being so terrified? [*A gesture in the direction of her son's room.*] I have no need to believe in ghosts. I know that he is alive for me. I'm not mad.

DONNA FIORINA: I know that! But, all the same, you're behaving as if you were!

DONN'ANNA: What do you know about how I'm behaving? What do you know about time as it is for me? Time as I live it? Those times when, upstairs in my room, I let my head fall back upon the pillows. I feel, I too feel the silence and the emptiness of these rooms . . . And there is no memory strong enough to give them life and fill them again for me . . . Because I'm tired. Then I too *know!* Yes, I too . . . *Know!* And a terrifying shudder runs through my body! *She* is my only refuge, therefore, my last remaining comfort . . . She who is coming, and who does not *know* as yet. The moment I think of her, she fills these rooms again, gives them back to life. I pour my whole self into her eyes and into her heart, so that I may still see him here before me. Still hear him. Still feel his living presence, here in this house. Because, you see, *that* is something which I can no longer do for myself!

DONNA FIORINA: But now that she's coming . . .

DONN'ANNA: You're trying to make me think about what's going to happen before it does indeed happen! Oh, how cruel you are! Can't you see how I'm suffering? I seem to myself to be like someone who takes each breath as if his very minutes here on earth were numbered. And you, you're trying to rob me of my last minute, and of my last breath!

DONNA FIORINA: But it's only because I consider that by coming over here like this she's risking compromising herself. *Now!* When everything's all over and done with.

DONN'ANNA: No. She's written to tell him . . . She's taking advantage of her husband's being away from home . . . He's out of Nice at the moment. Gone to Paris on business.

DONNA FIORINA: And suppose her husband were to come back unexpectedly and not find her there?

DONN'ANNA: She'll have given her mother some reason or other to excuse her absence to her husband. Her mother's still got her estate at Cortona ... She could have gone there for the few days that she'll have been here.

DONNA FIORINA: But what I say is ... How could she possibly have even *thought* of coming to join him here? *Here*. Under your very eyes?

DONN'ANNA: Why do you say *here* like that? It will be *I* who will bring her *here*. *She* wrote and asked him to meet her at the *station*.

DONNA FIORINA: And instead of him it'll be you she meets, h'm? And how will you tell her?

DONN'ANNA: First of all I shall ... I shall tell her to come with me. I can scarcely break the news to her just like that ... In the station ... In front of everybody.

DONNA FIORINA: But how do you think she'll feel at seeing you? What will she think at not finding *him* there to meet her?

DONN'ANNA: She'll think that he's not there because he's gone away. And that he's sent me to tell her. There you are ... That's what I'll tell her in the first instance ... Or something much of the same sort.

DONNA FIORINA: But afterwards, when you get back here ... Then at least you'll tell her everything, won't you? Everything, *won't* you?

DONN'ANNA: After I've persuaded her to come up here with me. Yes.

DONNA FIORINA: Then why are you putting out all these flowers?

DONN'ANNA: Because when she arrives here she still won't know! It's he who's doing all this! It's he, not I! Oh, please, for pity's sake don't make me talk about it! *She* is coming. And it is essential that these flowers should be here to greet her! [*Then, seeing* GIOVANNI *come in with the remaining flower-pot*] Down there, Giovanni, where I told you just now.

GIOVANNI [*having put the flower-pot down in the place appointed*]: That's the loveliest of the lot of them.

DONN'ANNA: Yes, we chose the most beautiful of them. And now go and tell them to get the carriage ready.

GIOVANNI: It's ready now, ma'am. In ten minutes you'll be at the station.

DONN'ANNA: Good. Good. You can go now. [GIOVANNI *goes out through the door Back.* DONN'ANNA, *a prey to her own growing impatience, goes over to the door Right and calls*] Elisabetta! Haven't you finished getting things ready yet?

DONNA FIORINA: But ...! But ... Anna! You're surely not putting her in there?

DONN'ANNA: No! It's not for her. I've told them to get a room ready for her upstairs. [*Then, going closer to the door Right, she calls more loudly*] Elisabetta! Why have you opened the window? [ELISABETTA *runs into the room. She begins to call out her message even before she is on stage.*]

ELISABETTA: The young master and the young mistress are back! [*Then, to* DONNA FIORINA] Your children are here, ma'am!

DONNA FIORINA [*in astonishment, and brimming over with joy*]: Lida? Flavio?

ELISABETTA: I heard them shouting in the garden! Oh yes, ma'am! They're running up the drive now!

DONN'ANNA: Your children ...

DONNA FIORINA: But ... How? ... What? ... They're a day early! They weren't due till tomorrow! [*And from off-stage can be heard cries of 'Mummy! Mummy!'*]

ELISABETTA: Here they are! Here they are!

[*And* LIDA *and* FLAVIO *burst into the room. She is about eighteen, he about twenty. Having left the country a year ago in order to study in town, they have now become quite, quite different – even in so short a space of time – from what they were before they went away. They are different not only in the way they think and in the way they feel, but in their very appearance . . . Their voices, their gestures, their every movement, the way they look at you, the way they smile . . . All are changed. They, naturally, aren't aware of this. Their mother, the first impetuous effusions of affection over, perceives it immediately. It leaves her utterly dismayed, for she is invaded by a tragic sense that here, suddenly and unexpectedly before her eyes, is proof evident of all that her sister has revealed to her.]*

LIDA [*running over to her mother and throwing her arms around her neck*]: Darling Mummy! Dear lovely darling Mummy! [*She kisses her.*]

DONNA FIORINA: My darling Lida! [*She kisses her.*] But how are you home so soon? Oh, Flavio! Flavio! [*She holds out her arms to him.*]

FLAVIO [*embracing her*]: Darling Mummy! [*He kisses her.*]

DONNA FIORINA: But . . . How? . . . What? Oh dear, how did you manage to get here so soon? Is it really you? To arrive just like this . . . !

LIDA: Oh, you see, we managed to get away today!

FLAVIO: It was a frantic rush! We got through everything in two hours flat!

LIDA: Oh yes, he can brag about it now! But he wasn't so keen to . . .

FLAVIO: I should jolly well think I wasn't! Run and do this for me! Dash along and do the other! Into the dressmaker's . . . On to the milliner's . . . *Chypre* Coty . . . Silk stockings! . . . What on earth you're going to do with them here in the country, I just can't imagine!

LIDA: Oh, Mummy, you must see the lots and lots of lovely things I've brought back with me! And some of them are for you too!

DONNA FIORINA [*she has tried to smile, as she has been listening to them; but, despite her efforts, she has felt herself, as it were, freezing from the moment when she suddenly became aware of how changed they were.* DONN'ANNA, *meanwhile, has withdrawn a little to one side, into the shadow that has begun to invade the room. Now, her eyes turned towards her sister,* DONNA FIORINA *says*]: Yes . . . Yes . . . But . . . Oh, my God! . . . I don't know . . . How can you go on talking like that . . . ?

[*And immediately* LIDA *and* FLAVIO – *for their gaze has followed their mother's* – *remember that they are in their aunt's house. They think of the misfortune that has so recently befallen her, and which they'd completely forgotten in the impetus of their first arrival; and, setting their mother's dismay down to this forgetfulness of theirs, they're upset and turn in confusion and self-reproach to their aunt.*]

FLAVIO: Oh, yes! Of course! . . . Aunt Anna . . .

LIDA: Oh, do forgive us, Aunt Anna! We came in in such a frantic hurry . . .

FLAVIO: And we hadn't seen Mummy for a whole year . . .

LIDA: Poor Fulvio . . .

FLAVIO: . . . we were so terribly sorry . . .

LIDA: . . . for you, Aunt Anna!

FLAVIO: I was banking on finding him here. Spending the vacation with him . . .

LIDA: And I was hoping to get to know him, because . . .

FLAVIO: But you must *remember* him! . . .

LIDA: . . . I was only nine when he went away . . . Only just, too!

FLAVIO: Poor Aunt Anna!

LIDA: Do forgive us! And you too, Mummy!

DONN'ANNA: No, Flavio. No, Lida. It's not on my account . . . It's on yours.

LIDA [*not understanding*]: *What's* on our account?

DONN'ANNA: Nothing, my dear children! [*She looks at them for a moment or so, then she kisses them on the forehead, first one then the other.*] Welcome home. [*She goes over to her sister and in an almost inaudible voice says with a smile – so as to comfort her*] Just think of this, my dear . . . At least they're more handsome now . . . And now it would be best if I were to go. [*Exit through the door Back. The others remain where they are for a moment or so, in silence – as if somehow suspended. The darkness continues gradually to invade the room.*]

FLAVIO: When we rushed in like that we didn't think . . .

LIDA: But what did she mean by 'it's on our account'?

DONNA FIORINA [*rousing herself, as if from a nightmare*]: No-thing! Nothing, my children! It's not true! No! No! . . . Let me look at you!

ELISABETTA: How they've changed!

DONNA FIORINA [*again it is as if she were rousing herself from a nightmare*]: They're ever so much more handsome! Much more handsome!

ELISABETTA [*gazing admiringly at* LIDA]: Oh yes, they most certainly are! Why, she's a grown-up young lady already! You'd never recognize her for the same girl!

DONNA FIORINA [*vehemently, gathering her daughter in her arms again, as if seeking to protect her*]: No, they're still the same as they were! Oh, my darling Lida! Lida darling! [*And immediately turning to her son*] My own dear Flavio!

FLAVIO [*again embracing her*]: But, Mummy dear, what's the matter?

DONNA FIORINA: Let me look at you! Let me have a good look at you! [*She takes* LIDA*'s face between her hands.*] Don't give it another thought! Look at me!

LIDA: But how did he die, Mummy? Why? Was it because of . . .

FLAVIO: . . . that woman?

DONNA FIORINA [*hurriedly – she is vexed*]: No! He fell ill quite suddenly, quite unexpectedly. I'll tell you about it later! Now tell me all about yourselves . . . I'd much rather talk about you . . . !

FLAVIO [*to* LIDA]: There, you see? It wasn't true. I told you it was all your usual romantic stuff and nonsense! If he was able to tear himself away from her, it's a pretty clear indication that all that terrific passion, that passion which was so great that he must inevitably die of it . . .

DONNA FIORINA: Why, *no*! What on earth are you talking about?

FLAVIO: I warn you, Mummy . . . She does nothing but read silly romantic novels!

DONNA FIORINA: Do you, Lida darling?

LIDA: Don't you believe him, Mummy dear! It's not true!

FLAVIO: She's brought at least twenty with her this time! Just think of that!

LIDA: Will you please do me the kindness of not interfering in my affairs?

DONNA FIORINA: But . . . What's this? You two . . . *Quarrelling*?

LIDA: Oh, he's insufferable! Don't take any notice of him, Mummy!

FLAVIO: May one know which heroine it was who prompted you to go in for *Chypre*?

DONNA FIORINA [*anguishedly, to herself*]: *Chypre*? . . . What is this *Chypre*? . . .

LIDA: It was a friend of mine who recommended it to me!

FLAVIO: Rosi?

LIDA: Pooh! *Rosi*!

FLAVIO: Franchi?

LIDA: Pooh! *Franchi*!

FLAVIO: She changes them at the rate of one a day! *Weather-hen*!

ELISABETTA: When they went away they were just like a simple little shepherd and shepherdess . . . And now . . . Why, the Good Lord save us, they're like a young lord and lady!

DONNA FIORINA [*again trying to react*]: Of course! Living in town . . . They've grown up and . . . [*Then, to* LIDA] Tell me . . . What *is* this *Chypre*?

FLAVIO: It's a perfume, Mummy darling – ninety lire for a tiny little bottle!

DONNA FIORINA: Perfume? A child like you, *use perfume* . . .?

LIDA: Mummy darling, I'm *eighteen*!

FLAVIO: Three little bottles – two hundred and seventy lire!

LIDA: And what about all the money *you've* spent on yourself? What with *ties* and *collars* and *gloves* . . . Heaven only knows how much you've spent! *I* don't! And then you've got the brazen impudence to tick me off for buying three miserable little bottles of *Chypre*!

DONNA FIORINA: Sh! Please be quiet! I can't bear to hear you talking like this! [*Then, to* LIDA, *her voice caressing*] You do your hair like this now, do you? Just like a grown-up young woman . . .

ELISABETTA: And when she went away it was hanging down her back in plaits!

DONNA FIORINA [*without listening to* ELISABETTA]: Yes, and look! You're taller than I am! [*Then, as if in dismay*] And how do I seem to you?

LIDA: You look very nice, Mummy darling! Ever so, ever so nice!

DONNA FIORINA: Then why are you looking at me like that?

LIDA: How am I looking at you?

DONNA FIORINA: I don't know . . . And you too, Flavio . . .

FLAVIO: You know, Mummy, you're being very strange! [*And he laughs as he looks at her.*]

DONNA FIORINA: No! No! Don't laugh like that! I beg you!

FLAVIO: Yes, I know one oughtn't to be laughing here. But the way you're talking . . . The way you're looking at us . . . It's so very strange . . .

DONNA FIORINA: The way I'm . . . ? [*Frantically*] It's got quite dark in here. I have to peer at you because I can hardly see you if I don't. [*And in fact the darkness has deepened. Gradually too the reflected light of the setting sun has become brighter and brighter in the dead son's room.*]

ELISABETTA: Wait a moment. I'll light the lamp.

DONNA FIORINA: No. Let's go home. Let's go home, children! Let's leave here . . . It's getting late.

LIDA [*as she turns round she notices the glow of light in the other room*]: Oh, there's a light in that room. Who's in there?

DONNA FIORINA: If you only knew!

FLAVIO [*quietly, standing quite still*]: Was it in there that he died?

ELISABETTA [*sombrely, after a silence*]: In here it's as if *we were no longer alive* . . . As if only *he* was alive.

FLAVIO: Does she keep a light burning for him?

LIDA [*who has come timorously nearer in order to have a look*]: And the room . . . Just as it was?

DONNA FIORINA: Don't look, Lida!

FLAVIO: Just as though he were due back at any minute?

ELISABETTA: No, just as though he'd never gone away at all. Just as though he was still here. And the same man that he was before he ever went away. She says she'll see to it that he never *does* go away. [*There is a short pause and then she adds in a sombre tone*] Because when children go away they die for their mother. They're no longer what they were . . . *Before!* [*In the darkness and the silence – which are like the darkness and the silence of a nightmare that has overtaken them all –* DONNA FIORINA *bursts into subdued weeping.*]

FLAVIO [*for a moment his mother's weeping is the only sound to be heard, as it trembles through that deathly silence; then* FLAVIO, *mistakenly attributing his mother's tears to the grief she feels on her sister's account, says*]: Poor Aunt Anna! How she must be suffering!

LIDA: Is it like a kind of madness?

ELISABETTA: She talks about him in such a way that it almost makes you see him. When I'm alone in here I keep looking back over my shoulder . . . Half expecting him to come out of this room and go out through that door and into the garden. Or go over to the window. I live in a constant tremble. She insists on me keeping his room neat and tidy. I have to make the bed every day. Look! You can see for yourself . . . It's all turned down. Every evening the same routine. Everything ready. Just as if he was coming in to go to bed.

DONNA FIORINA [LIDA, *terrified by* ELISABETTA'*s words, has instinctively flung herself into her mother's arms, pressing herself close to her. In a low voice – the voice of a beggar –* DONNA FIORINA *says*]: Darling Lida! My own darling Lida, you do still love me, don't you?

LIDA [*all intent on what* ELISABETTA *is saying, she pays no heed to her mother's words*]: So she goes on . . .

ELISABETTA: . . . making him live!

DONNA FIORINA [*at the end of her tether; as if her heart were bursting from out of her breast*]: Flavio! My children! Let's leave this house! Let's go home, *for pity's sake!*

ELISABETTA: Wait just a moment, ma'am. I'll give you a light. It's pitch dark out there. Nobody's lit up yet.

DONNA FIORINA: Yes. Thank you, Elisabetta. Let's go! Let's get away from here!

[ELISABETTA *goes out first. She is followed by* DONNA FIORINA, LIDA, *and* FLAVIO – *in that order. The stage remains dark and empty, the only patch of light being that spectral glow which points an ever-lengthening finger through the door Right. There is a long pause. Then, and without making the faintest noise, the chair that is drawn up in front of the writing-desk slowly moves away from the desk, just as if an invisible hand were twisting it away. After another pause – a shorter one this time – the light curtain which masks the window is lifted a little to one side, as if twitched back by the same hand; then it falls once again into position. For who knows what sort of things happen – all unseen by anyone – in the shadowy darkness of deserted rooms where someone has died? Shortly afterwards* ELISABETTA *comes back in again, immediately lighting up the room. Instinctively she pushes the chair back to its former position by the writing-table, without having the slightest suspicion that someone has moved it. Then, so as to get out of sight of the things in the room, she goes over to the window. She too lifts the light curtain to one side with her hand; then she opens the window and looks out into the garden.*]

ELISABETTA [*from the window*]: Who's that there? [*Pause.*] Oh! It's you, is it, Giovanni? [*Pause.*] Giovanni?

GIOVANNI'S VOICE [*happily, coming from the garden*]: Can you see it?

ELISABETTA: No. What?

GIOVANNI'S VOICE: Over there! You can still see it. Between the olive trees. Up there on the hill!

ELISABETTA: Ah, yes! Yes, I can see it! But what are you doing, standing there staring up at the moon?

GIOVANNI'S VOICE: I want to see if it's true what he said to me.

ELISABETTA: What *who* said to you?

GIOVANNI'S VOICE: What do you mean *who*? Why, *him*! Him that can't see it any more for himself.

ELISABETTA: Ah, *him*?

GIOVANNI'S VOICE: He was there when he said it... Where you are now.

ELISABETTA: Don't! You're giving me the creeps! And I've had just about as much as I can stand!

GIOVANNI'S VOICE: It was the night after he got back.

ELISABETTA: And he talked to you about the moon? What did he say?

GIOVANNI'S VOICE: The higher it goes, the more it vanishes.

ELISABETTA: The moon?

GIOVANNI'S VOICE: You look around you, at things here on earth... He said to me... And you see the light up there on the hill. Or down here on these plants. But if you lift up your head and look at the moon itself . . . Well, the higher it is the more you see it as something ever so far away from our night here.

ELISABETTA: Far away? Why far away?

GIOVANNI'S VOICE: Because night is down here *with us*. But the moon can't see it. Can't see our night. Because it's up there, lost in its own light. Do you understand? *Vanished* into its own light. I wonder what it was he was thinking about. Eh? When he was looking up at the moon that night. Oh, I can hear the carriage-bells.

ELISABETTA: Quick, then! Run along and open the gate!

[ELISABETTA *hastily closes the window and goes out through the door Back. Shortly afterwards* LUCIA MAUBEL *and* DONN'ANNA *come in through this same door. During the journey up from the station* DONN'ANNA *has – as in the first scene she said she would – started to explain things to* LUCIA. *The young woman is deeply wounded, thoroughly perturbed and most hurt by what she has been told.*]

DONN'ANNA [*anxiously, as she shows her in*]: Come in. Come in. These are his rooms. You'll soon see that for yourself, if you go in there. You'll see yourself everywhere about the room. In everything. In the last flowers he left standing in front of all the pictures of you, when he went away yesterday.

LUCIA [*her voice friendly but ironical*]: Flowers . . . And then he ran away?

DONN'ANNA: Are you going to start reproaching him again? If you only knew what it cost him not to be here . . .

LUCIA: I come to join him, and he's nowhere to be found. And you say it's for my sake that he's done this?

DONN'ANNA: Quite against the promptings of his heart! . . .

LUCIA: Out of prudence? And doesn't such great prudence on his part seem to you very much more than a mere reproof . . . A downright affront to me? . . . An insult . . . ?

DONN'ANNA [*sorrowingly*]: No! No!

LUCIA: Oh, my God! An insult! And so cruel that it almost drives one to think that all his prudence was on his own account! Not on *mine*!

DONN'ANNA: No! No! It *was* on your account! It was on your account that he . . . !

LUCIA: But I'm not dead! I'm *here*!

DONN'ANNA: Dead? Why do you say that? What are you talking about?

LUCIA: Oh, yes! Forgive me, but . . . ! If the moment I arrive here he runs away, leaving flowers in front of the pictures of me . . . Well, what does it all mean? That he wants his love to be like the love he would have for a dead woman? And I've left behind all that other life of mine, just so as to hasten here to join him! Oh! Oh, it's horrible! What he's done is horrible! [*She buries her face in her hands, her body trembling with shame and with angry disdain.*]

DONN'ANNA [*almost to herself, gazing into vacancy*]: He wouldn't have done it . . . He certainly wouldn't have done it . . .

LUCIA [*suddenly turning and looking at her*]: So there *is* a reason why he's acted as he has?

DONN'ANNA [*almost inaudibly*]: Yes. [*And a dreary smile comes to her lips.*]

LUCIA: And what is it? Tell me!

DONN'ANNA: May I call you Lucia?

LUCIA: Yes, do call me Lucia. As a matter of fact, I'm grateful to you for wanting to.

DONN'ANNA: And will you also let me tell you that he didn't intend to insult you when . . . When he had to leave . . .

LUCIA: But tell me *why*! What was the reason?

DONN'ANNA: I'll tell you . . . This is how it was . . . But first of all there's this . . . He had no intention of insulting you when he entrusted you to my care . . .

LUCIA: Oh, no! Please don't misunderstand me! . . . I . . . I know very well that . . .

DONN'ANNA: . . . that he always confided in me about everything . . . About how deeply you were in love with one
another . . . Everything . . .

LUCIA [*her face darkening*]: Everything?

DONN'ANNA: He could confide everything in me because . . .

LUCIA [*it is as if a shudder runs throughout her body; once more
she buries her face in her hands; and, her whole body racked with
her torment, she shakes her head in denial of what* DONN'ANNA
is saying.]

DONN'ANNA [*looking at her, pale and confused*]: No?

LUCIA [*more with a gesture of her head than with her actual
words; she is very near to tears*]: No . . . No . . .

DONN'ANNA [*pale and confused; still gazing at her*]: But . . .
How? . . . What? . . . Then . . .

LUCIA [*bursts out with*]: Oh, forgive me! Forgive me! Be my
mother too! That's why I came here!

DONN'ANNA: But in that case he . . .

LUCIA: . . . came away from me for that very reason!

DONN'ANNA: But wasn't it you who forced him to come
away and leave you?

LUCIA: Yes! Yes, it was I! But, *afterwards! Afterwards!* In the
end our love betrayed us! Our love, which had remained
a pure love for so many years, finally overthrew us
both!

DONN'ANNA: Ah, so that's why . . . ?

LUCIA: In an absolute frenzy of distraction and terror I forced
him to come away from me. I should never have been able
to look my children in the face again. But it was useless,
useless. I *couldn't* look them in the face again. I felt just as
if I were dying. [*She looks at her, her eyes dreadful to behold
in their suffering.*] Do you realize why? . . . There's another
child in my womb now! [*And she hides her face.*]

DONN'ANNA: *His* child?

LUCIA: That's why I came here.

DONN'ANNA: *His* . . . Child? *His child?*

LUCIA: He doesn't know yet! But he must be told! Tell me where he is!

DONN'ANNA: Oh, my daughter! My daughter! So he really *is* alive in you? When he parted from you he left within you ... *A life* ... *His* life ... Didn't he?

LUCIA: Yes! Yes! But he must know at once! Where is he? Oh, tell me! Where is he?

DONN'ANNA: Oh, how can I possibly tell you ... *Now?* Oh, my God! Oh, my God! How can I possibly tell you now?

LUCIA: Why can't you tell me? Don't you know?

DONN'ANNA: He's gone away ...

LUCIA: But didn't he tell you where he was going?

DONN'ANNA: He didn't tell me.

LUCIA: I see how it was ... He suspected that ... That it was only because ... [*She breaks off with an exclamation of anger.*] But it wasn't right of him to suspect me of *that*! Oh yes, I was just as guilty as he was! I wanted it too! But afterwards I forced him to come away. And if I could possibly have helped myself, even *this* wouldn't have brought me here now! But I can't go on any longer! Not *now*! I can't tear myself away from him now! I can't go back ... *There* ... Not in my present condition ... The very thought of it fills me with horror!

DONN'ANNA: No, of course you can't! You're quite right!

LUCIA: Can't you ... ? *Really and truly* ... ? *Can't* you tell me where he is? Do you mean to say you really don't know? But how can we tell him about ... *This?*

DONN'ANNA: Just wait a moment! Wait just a moment! Yes, we'll find a way of letting him know ...

LUCIA: But *how?* And *where?* If you don't know where he is? He'd hardly have gone off on a long trip without telling you ... And giving *me* some sort of warning!

DONN'ANNA: No! No! ... He's probably not very far away ... He *can't* be far away ...

LUCIA: He was afraid that if he left word even with you about where he was going ... But perhaps it was *you* who advised him to go away?

DONN'ANNA: I didn't know ...

LUCIA [*she presses a hand over her eyes*]: Oh, I'm getting so suspicious! Oh, how sad it all is! I know, I ought to have written and told him about the child. But I didn't want to waste all my strength in words, at a time when I'd need all that strength to carry out what I was resolved to do. What I've now done! He thought I was just being foolish and hysterical ...

DONN'ANNA [*to calm her*]: There! There! ...

LUCIA: And so he ran away! So that I should find my true self again in you ... Come to my senses again. Yes, I understand. I understand. [*Abruptly changing tone.*] Will he come back? Will he write to you? Will he let you know where he is?

DONN'ANNA: Yes! Yes, of course he will! Now calm yourself! Come and sit down! *Here*. Sit down beside me. And let me call you *my daughter* ...

LUCIA: Yes ... Yes ...

DONN'ANNA: Lucia ...

LUCIA: Yes ...

DONN'ANNA: My daughter!

LUCIA: Yes, Mummy! *Mummy!* Now I feel that it's all for the best that things should have turned out the way they have. That I should have met you here first, and not him ...

DONN'ANNA: Oh, my dear lovely daughter! Yes, you *are* lovely! These beautiful eyes ... Your brow ... The fragrance of your hair ... Yes, I can understand! It's so easy to understand why ... ! Yes, he couldn't help but ... But he should have made you his right from the very first moment! From the very first moment you loved one another! He owed me this joy! It was his duty to give this joy to me ...

The joy of having . . . In you . . . Another child . . . A *daughter* ! . . . Just as you are now . . . Just as you are now . . .

LUCIA: Without all the evil we've committed . . . Oh, my God! The *harm* we've done!

DONN'ANNA: You mustn't think about that now! Who is there that knows, my daughter, how much evil is done to others by those who have *not* sinned! Of how much evil committed by those who *have* sinned *they* are the cause. The sinful are perhaps the only ones who will be rewarded with good come of evil. You are in a better position to know that than I am.

LUCIA: I've cut my life into two . . . I . . .

DONN'ANNA: You have a life within you . . .

LUCIA: But what about *them*? My *other* children! There at home! I was obliged to fly here, with *this* . . . Something that is still nothing! And yet it's something that has suddenly become *everything*! The whole of our love spilled out in a sudden overwhelming torrent . . . And became in that sudden instant something that it should never have become!

DONN'ANNA: Life!

LUCIA: Oh, you don't know what I've suffered! You could never possibly imagine what I've been through! The very bed in which you're resting! Oh, my God! It becomes a thing of horror! There were certain things I'd sworn to myself that I'd never let happen . . . You know how some cuts can smart terribly, don't you? . . . It was just like that! . . . I lay there . . . My teeth clenched . . . Resisting till I could resist no more . . . Trying to prevent my body from ceasing to belong to me . . . Trying to prevent it from yielding! And every so often I'd burst out of that horrible nightmare, where for one blind fleeting moment I'd been forced to be untrue to the promises I'd made myself . . . Oh, yes! *Free!* A free woman! Freed from their bondage! I could be his . . . In all the fullness of my purity . . .

THE LIFE I GAVE YOU

Because of the martyrdom that I'd suffered! . . . *His* . . .
And without remorse. But we shouldn't have yielded our
bodies to one another! What I had sworn to myself was
valid only so long as our love remained chaste . . . Because,
those other children too . . . The ones I've left there at
home . . . What do you think I . . . ? You're a mother, and
I can talk to you about . . .

DONN'ANNA: . . . Yes . . . Tell me . . . Tell me . . .

LUCIA: Those other children . . . Well, the truth is . . . Those
children were not born of a love that had been made flesh.
They were *his* children . . . Flesh of my husband's flesh . . .
But the love that I had poured into them, the love that I
had given even to those other children of mine . . . I . . .
I . . . My heart was so full of the man I loved . . . That it
was as if I'd made even them *his* children. Love is one and
indivisible! . . . And now . . . Now . . . Such a love is no
longer possible! . . . I can't belong to two men! I'd kill
myself sooner!

DONN'ANNA: No, you can't belong to them both. Not only
for your own sake, but also because you mustn't give that
other man this scrap of life which belongs to you and to
him, and to you two alone . . .

LUCIA: Do you really think that? *Do* you?

DONN'ANNA: You mustn't go back to him! [*For a moment
she falters.*] I beg you not to . . .

LUCIA: But you've already told me I mustn't!

DONN'ANNA: Yes . . . So as to find out whether you'd really
thought about this aspect of things!

LUCIA [*after a brief pause, collecting herself; her face darkens*]: The
violence I've done to myself throughout so many years . . .
Those two children who have been born to me in spite of
that violence . . . [*She suddenly breaks off.*]

DONN'ANNA: What do you mean?

LUCIA: Nothing . . . Nothing against them! Oh, but my
loathing for *him*! It's such an obscure, intimate feeling of

hate . . . I don't know how to put it into words . . . I feel
as if I'd twice become a mother . . . Well, *without playing
the slightest part in my children's creation*! I was merely
material to be worked by a man who was an utter stranger
to me. And, what is more, these children were wrought in
my living flesh, formed in the tearing agony of my soul!
Whilst he . . . *He!* . . . Oh, he wouldn't even have known
whether this child was his or not!

DONN'ANNA: But *you* know!

LUCIA: Yes. And I've acted as I have . . . I've made my
decision . . . Out of respect for myself . . . Not out of any
consideration for him! The wrong that I'd have done him
would have been less by far than the wrong that he's done
me!

DONN'ANNA: I don't know him. I can't judge.

LUCIA: He made me a mother merely because I was his wife.
So that he could go blithely on his way with other
women . . . Woman after woman! . . . Hundreds of them!
. . . Feeling nothing but contempt for them and for me!
Oh, he's a cynic! He thinks of nothing but his business . . .
Outside business he's the most inane and frigid creature
alive! He looks at life merely in order to laugh at it. He
looks on women as just so many sacrifices to his lust, and
on men as so many fools to be cheated and deceived. I was
able to put up with him, to go on living with him, only
because I had someone who held me up . . . Who gave me
a purer air to breathe, outside that world of brutish ugliness.
But we shouldn't have become brute beasts ourselves! I
swear, I swear there was no joy in it for me! And as proof
of what I say, there's . . . Oh, it's a horrible thing to say!
But that's how it is for me! . . . The proof of my joylessness
lies in this . . . In my being a mother once again.

DONN'ANNA: Oh, God! No! What are you saying?

LUCIA: I came here so that he might make me feel that it's
not true . . . If he can! For the last three years I've done

everything possible to avoid having another child. I believe ... Yes, I too believe that there should be joy in the begetting and the bearing of a child. And there is only one thing that I want. I swear to you that there is only one thing that I want now! I want the bearing of this child to become for me ... Really and truly to *be*! ... The joy that I have never yet experienced!

DONN'ANNA: But that joy, my daughter, is something which you must have in your heart! If you haven't got that joy in your heart, who can possibly give it to you?

LUCIA: *He* can! *He* can!

DONN'ANNA: Yes ... *He* can. But only in so far as you have *him* in your heart too! Only if *that* is true. That's how it is ... *Always!* Don't seek for anything that doesn't come to you from within yourself.

LUCIA: What do you think can possibly come to me from within myself at this moment? Oh, I'm so bewildered by everything ... In such a state of suspense! His betraying me ... By not being here to meet me ... I need him! I need to see him! Speak with him! Hear his voice! ... Where is he? Where do you think he's likely to have gone? How will he find out about the child? I shan't have a moment's rest until he *does* know! Do you really mean to say that you haven't the vaguest idea, that you can't imagine where he might have gone?

DONN'ANNA: I don't know where he's gone, my daughter. But now you must give yourself a little peace ...

LUCIA: I can't!

DONN'ANNA: You're trembling all over. You're so very tired! It's been a long journey!

LUCIA: There's a buzzing in my ears ... My head's swimming ...

DONN'ANNA: You see?

LUCIA: All this terrible worry! All this worry!

DONN'ANNA: You must go and rest ...

LUCIA: And then not to find him! . . . I feel feverish.

DONN'ANNA: What you need is a good rest. We'll think about what to do . . . Tomorrow.

LUCIA: Oh, I shall go mad before this night is out!

DONN'ANNA: No . . . Look . . . I'll teach you how not to go mad. It's what one does when someone is far, far away. It's what I did for a long time . . . All the time that he was away . . . With you. I felt him near me because I *made* him be near me. Made him in my heart! No, he wasn't just *near* me. I had him here, held deep within my heart! You must do the same. And then this night will pass away. Just remember that these are his rooms. Think of him as in there . . .

LUCIA: Does he sleep in there?

DONN'ANNA: Yes . . . In there. And it's on that table that he writes to you . . .

LUCIA: Oh, the horrible things he's written to me!

DONN'ANNA: And do you see this bench? Right up till he went away yesterday he'd sit on here and talk to me about you . . . Oh, the hundreds and hundreds of things he's told me! . . .

LUCIA: And then he went away . . .

DONN'ANNA: He didn't *know*! Oh, the countless things he's told me! So that I should be able to make you understand without hurting you, and without causing you to suffer the pain that comes from his having gone away for your sake.

LUCIA: But now . . .

DONN'ANNA: Ah, yes! *Now!* You're quite right. Everything's changed . . . Now that you have this child within your womb . . .

LUCIA: He'll come back again!

DONN'ANNA: He'll come back again. Don't you worry! He'll come back again. But now, come on upstairs with me! Come on! . . . I've got a room ready for you upstairs.

LUCIA: I want to see his room.

DONN'ANNA: Yes, of course you may. Come along . . . Do go in.

LUCIA: You wouldn't let me stay down here, would you?

DONN'ANNA: You mean . . . You want to stay down here, in his rooms?

LUCIA: Now I *can* stay with him. And he is still with me.

DONN'ANNA: You see? You see? You're beginning to feel it already! Yes, sleep in here if you want to, my daughter!

LUCIA [*going into the other room*]: Perhaps it's better like this . . . Nearer . . .

DONN'ANNA: Yes! In your heart! In your heart!

[*She follows her into the other room. For a moment or so the stage remains empty. From the other room you can hear the confused murmur of their two voices as they talk together. They're not sad; on the contrary, there is a marked gaiety in their tones. And* LUCIA *may even give a laugh – as if she were surprised by something. Then* DONN'ANNA *comes out, her face turned towards the room she is leaving. She is talking all the while to the younger woman, who accompanies her as far as the threshold.*]

LUCIA [*happily, standing on the threshold*]: Yes, and a lovely moonlight night too!

DONN'ANNA: Good night, my dear! See you in the morning. I'll close the door.

LUCIA [*retiring into the other room*]: Good night!

DONN'ANNA [*she is now on her own; she closes the door, and stands before it for a moment or so, as if exhausted; then her whole face lights up and is resplendent with a spasm of divine joy; and, more with her eyes than with her lips, she says*]: He's alive!

E

ACT THREE

The scene is the same as in the previous Acts. It is early the following morning.

[*Shortly after the curtain goes up,* GIOVANNI *appears in the doorway Back. He stands to one side to usher in* MRS FRANCESCA NORETTI. *She has just arrived from the station, in a state of great anxiety, anguish, and dismay.*]

GIOVANNI: Do come in! Do come in, ma'am.

FRANCESCA: But how can she possibly sleep?

GIOVANNI: She's probably tired out after her journey. Besides, it's only just gone seven.

FRANCESCA: Whereabouts is she sleeping? Don't you know?

GIOVANNI: Elisabetta got a room ready for her yesterday on the floor above this.

FRANCESCA: Can't you take me to her?

GIOVANNI: I don't go upstairs in the house, ma'am. But I've asked them to tell Elisabetta. And the mistress is up already. I saw her when she opened her window, round about sunrise.

FRANCESCA: But is it possible that she still doesn't know that he's dead? She got here yesterday evening, did you say?

GIOVANNI: Yes, ma'am, yesterday evening. The mistress went to fetch her from the station.

FRANCESCA: And you saw her arrive? Was she crying?

GIOVANNI: No, ma'am. Didn't seem to be to me.

FRANCESCA: I wonder if they can't have told her yet, then? Because for her to sleep . . .

GIOVANNI: Oh, that's quite probable, ma'am, because . . . Well, look at these flowers. I brought them in myself, yesterday evening. It's just as if he wasn't dead for the mistress. She's not even put on black for him.

FRANCESCA: And it's for that reason that she's not told anybody anything about his death, is it? It was eleven days ago that he died, m'm?

GIOVANNI: This very morning.

FRANCESCA: I heard about it the moment I arrived at the station . . . When I asked for him . . . Asked where he lived . . .

GIOVANNI: Here's the mistress now. [DONN'ANNA *enters quickly, and* GIOVANNI *goes out.*]

DONN'ANNA: Please speak more quietly! Sh! For pity's sake! . . . You're her mother?

FRANCESCA: You can just imagine what a state I'm in, Donn'Anna! I'm absolutely out of my mind with . . . All the time I've been travelling here I've been . . . Where is she? Where is she? . . . Does she still not know?

DONN'ANNA: Sh! Quietly! *Quietly!* No, she doesn't know.

FRANCESCA: Take me to her! I'll wake her up and tell her myself!

DONN'ANNA: No, Mrs Noretti, no! For pity's sake don't!

FRANCESCA: But, why not? And you . . . Not to tell anybody, not even me, about your misfortune! If you'd only told me, I could have prevented her from doing the mad thing she's done!

DONN'ANNA: It wasn't on his account that she did what she did. No! Believe me!

FRANCESCA: It *wasn't* on his account? What do you mean?

DONN'ANNA: No. No. I'll tell you . . .

FRANCESCA: I want to see her . . . *At once!*

DONN'ANNA: But since you know now, you mustn't be afraid any longer, Mrs Noretti . . . You must stop being so terribly anxious . . .

FRANCESCA: But how do you expect me *not* to be anxious? *Not* to be afraid? I . . .

DONN'ANNA: Now, keep calm! Just let me tell you . . .

FRANCESCA: I shall be worried to death until I've got her

back home! I rushed out of the house the moment I got the note she left me, asking me to take care of the children. She's got two children . . . Did you know that? Oh, God, how it is that I'm not dead, I just don't know!

DONN'ANNA: Sh! Please be quiet! . . . Come with me . . . Please! . . . She's asleep in there!

FRANCESCA: Oh! In there? I'll go in to her at once.

[*Makes as if to hurl herself in the direction of the door Right.*]

DONN'ANNA [*blocking her way*]: No, Mrs Noretti! You don't know the terrible harm you'd be doing! [*There is such a strange note in her voice as she utters this admonition that* FRANCESCA *remains poised for a moment in dismay, almost overwhelmed, in fact.*]

FRANCESCA: Why?

DONN'ANNA [*immediately, decisively*]: Because you don't know what I know! The case is very much more serious than you imagine!

FRANCESCA: More serious? [*She looks at her in terror.*]

DONN'ANNA: Yes! She told me all about . . . *It* . . . Last night when she arrived.

FRANCESCA: That . . . That . . . She . . . They'd been . . .

DONN'ANNA: Yes. And that he's not so dead as you think he is.

FRANCESCA [*stammering, terrified*]: What do you mean?

DONN'ANNA: I mean . . . Well, if he's now alive in her . . . Just as the love of a man can always come alive, can always become life itself, within a woman . . . When he makes her a mother . . . Do you understand what I mean?

FRANCESCA [*in horror*]: Your son? Oh, God! And how . . . ? But in that case . . . ! So that's why . . . ?

DONN'ANNA: She was in such a state of desperation when she got here that it just wasn't possible for me to . . . 'To tell her all about it.' I told her that he'd gone away . . . Out of consideration for her . . . Out of prudence . . . So as not to compromise her. Even that much was quite sufficient to make her see herself as a dead woman ... To make her feel that she was dead ...

FRANCESCA: That *she* was dead?

DONN'ANNA: Yes, of course, that *she* was dead. Dead in his heart! So I ask you ... How could we possibly bear to make him die for her now?

FRANCESCA: But before you ... Before you let her compromise herself by coming here, you ought to have told me that he was dead!

DONN'ANNA: Mrs Noretti, you should thank Heaven that I haven't *that* on my conscience! I feel no remorse for not having told you. At first I thought that I *did* feel remorse ... That I ought to feel it. But I was able to discern that on the contrary I was inspired by God when I sent that letter to your daughter ... The letter he left, and that I finished.

FRANCESCA [*in horror*]: But ... You mean to say? ... How ... ? After ... After he was dead?

DONN'ANNA: Remember, for your daughter, it's not a question of *after*! I tell you, it was a wonderful stroke of good fortune! It was a Heaven-sent inspiration! In the state of mind that she was in when she got here, she'd have ... And we'd have known nothing about it, you and I! Nothing! ... If she'd suddenly had him snatched away from her ... She'd have killed herself! Oh, believe me!

FRANCESCA: But you ... Oh, my God! Do you want to keep my daughter tied to a corpse for the rest of her life?

DONN'ANNA: How can you speak of a *corpse*? Death for her is *there*, there with the man to whom *you* bound her! That man, yes, *that* man is a corpse! I, on the other hand ... I've been trying to ... I began yesterday evening ... I've been trying to make her realize ...

FRANCESCA: That her other children are there, with him ...

DONN'ANNA: Oh, she knows that well enough! She told me about it herself. Oh, she was absolutely heartbroken! She told me things that sent shudders running through my whole body . . .

FRANCESCA: About her children?

DONN'ANNA: Yes. About how she'd made them hers after . . . Oh, long after! . . . They'd been born to her. After they'd been born as strangers to her. She'd been able to make them *her* children because of my son's love for her. Do you understand? They too had need of his love, if they were to become truly alive for her . . . And yet, as you've seen, she could leave them so as to come here.

FRANCESCA: But once she gets to know that he's no longer here . . .

DONN'ANNA: He must be here. Yes, he *must* be here . . . If you intend to drag her back with you to the martyrdom of her life with that man. And you too must make her realize, as I have tried to make her realize, in just what way he must be alive for her from now on. He must live in her heart alone. She mustn't seek to find him anywhere but in her heart. He'll live with the life that she will give him. That's how he'll be alive for her. But first of all we must promise her that she'll see him again. Do you understand?

FRANCESCA [*utterly astounded*]: That *she'll see him again?*

DONN'ANNA: Not *here*! 'He won't come back here,' we'll tell her, 'not until he knows that you're gone again. You'll see him very soon, because he'll come back to you . . . *There*.' There you are. Tell her that and maybe you'll be able to take her back with you. Remember – she's in there. Waiting for him. She wanted to sleep in his bed. Perhaps she's dreaming of him. The moment she wakes up, she'll think of him as a living man, a man who's just about to come back to her.

FRANCESCA [*as* DONN'ANNA *has been speaking,* FRANCESCA *has been gazing at her in terror, and with ever-increasing horror. Gradually her horror resolves itself into infinite compassion*]: Oh, my God, Donn'Anna! . . . This is madness!

[*At this moment the door Right opens, and* LUCIA *appears on the threshold. When she sees her mother looking and acting like this she is at first surprised and then perturbed. She looks at his mother and in a flash she understands intuitively that some disaster has occurred.*]

LUCIA: Oh! Mummy! *You? Here?* [*She starts to run towards her; then she stops and stands there, looking first at one, then at the other.*] What's the matter?

FRANCESCA [*she is trembling all over; there is no anxiety in her voice or bearing; she speaks in a tone that will help her daughter to understand*]: My daughter . . . My daughter . . .

LUCIA [*again that checked movement towards her; again that looking from one to the other*]: But what's happened? What were you talking about?

DONN'ANNA [*to repair the damage done by* FRANCESCA'*s words*]: Nothing. As you see, she's come to . . . She's come to find out about you . . .

LUCIA: That's not true! Why don't you say something, Mummy! . . . What's happened? [*Then, shrieking the words*] Tell me!

FRANCESCA [*rushing over to her, so as to embrace her*]: My daughter!

LUCIA: Is he dead? Is he dead? [*She repulses her mother's embrace and turns towards* DONN'ANNA.] No! Dead? But . . . How can he . . . ? You . . . No! It's not possible! Oh, my God! [*With her hands thrust into her hair*] That dream I had! [*She breaks off in dismay and looks around her.*] Dead? . . . Tell me! *Is* he dead? *Tell me!*

FRANCESCA: He died many days ago, my daughter . . .

LUCIA: *Many* days? [*Then, to* DONN'ANNA] He died many days ago? And you . . . But how *could* you? Why didn't you tell me? How did he die? *How did he die?* . . . Oh, God, did he die in there? In that room? Where I've been sleeping? And you persuaded me to sleep in there? [DONN'ANNA *remains utterly motionless, like a figure carved upon a sepulchre.*]

Yes, I myself wanted to sleep in there, but you . . . Oh, how could you? You talked about 'the flowers'. You told me, 'He's gone away . . . These are his rooms . . . I don't know where he's gone.' . . . And I dreamt about him. Dreamt that he could never come back again. Because he'd gone so far away. I could see him. And he was so far away. And there was death in his face. Oh, his face! His face! . . . Oh, God! Oh, God! [*And she bursts into tears, abandoning herself utterly to her grief.*] It was so as to stop me from wondering why he wasn't here, waiting for me . . . As he should have been . . . Why I didn't find him here . . . Yes! It was the only thing that could have happened! He was dead! And I didn't realize it, because you . . . [*Her sobs grow less intense, for now utter bewilderment is prevailing over her sorrow.*] But how could you do such a thing? How could you possibly bring yourself to do such a thing? . . . For my sake? And he's dead for you as well! It's incredible! You talked to me about him as if he were alive!

DONN'ANNA [*looking into the distance*]: I can see him . . .

LUCIA [*in stupefaction*]: And is he dead? *Isn't* he dead? Here and now? Lying dead beneath the gaze of your eyes?

DONN'ANNA: No. Now . . .

LUCIA: What do you mean, *now?* . . .

DONN'ANNA: Now . . . It is now that I can see him dying.

LUCIA: What do you . . . What are you talking about? [DONN'ANNA *covers her face with her hands.* LUCIA *cries out*] I knew! I knew he must be dead! I didn't want to believe it! He told me himself, last time he left me . . . He told me that he was coming here to die!

DONN'ANNA [*uncovering her face*]: And I didn't see it.

LUCIA: But *I* did! He was dying . . . Had been for years . . . The light in his eyes was quite extinguished . . . It was as if he was already dead when he left me! When I looked at him, he was so pale, so very pale . . . When I looked at him, he was so wretched, so very wretched. I knew at once that he must be dead!

DONN'ANNA: Yes, wretched ... And with the light in his eyes quite extinguished. Yes ... And become like ... Yes, changed ... Changed like this ... Now I can see him ... I can see him for you, my daughter. [*She draws her to her, in what is almost a terrifying shudder ... A shudder that with crashing suddenness strikes through her.*] Oh, my daughter! Yes ... Now ... Here in your flesh ... I can see him ... Dying ... Now I can feel the chill of his death ... Here ... Here in the scalding warmth of these tears of yours! ... Now you reveal him to me, just as he was ... In the terrible state that he was! I didn't see him! I could never have wept, because I never saw him! But now I *can* see him! Now I *can* see him!

LUCIA [*gradually she has released herself from* DONN'ANNA'*s embrace and retreated, as if in horror, till she is very close to her mother*]: Oh, my God! What are you saying? What are you saying?

DONN'ANNA [*alone*]: Oh, my son! Your dear body! You went away like that ... So wretched! So utterly wretched! And I ... I embalmed you ... *Alive!* I embalmed the living you ... You as you no longer were ... As you could no longer be ... With that dear hair ... And those eyes that you'd lost ... Those eyes that could never laugh for you again! And because they could never laugh for you again, I didn't recognize them as your eyes! ... And then ... What did I do? Did I try to make you live a life that was beyond the frontiers of your life? Beyond the confines of the life that had consumed you? Oh, poor, poor flesh of my flesh ... My son whom I never saw again! Whom I shall never see again! ... Where are you? [*She turns and looks around her, seeking him.*] Where are you?

LUCIA [*running over to her*]: Here, Mummy!

DONN'ANNA [*standing stock-still for a fraction of a moment*]:

You? [*Then, with a loud cry*] Yes! Oh, yes! [*Frantically she embraces her.*] Don't take him away with you! Don't go away! Don't go away!

LUCIA: No, I shan't go away! I shan't go away, Mummy. I shan't go away!

FRANCESCA: What do you mean, *you won't go away*? What are you talking about? You're coming with me! And this very moment!

DONN'ANNA: No! Leave her with me, Mrs Noretti! She's mine! *Mine!* Leave her with me! You must leave me . . . Her!

FRANCESCA: But you're mad, Donn'Anna!

DONN'ANNA: Remember . . . What she has done to me is a terrible crime against me! A terrible crime! [*Then, at once, to* LUCIA, *in a caressing voice*] No! No! . . . You do realize, don't you? . . . I'm not blaming you! . . . I am your mother!

FRANCESCA: Do you mean you want her to desert me for you? And leave her children? [*To* LUCIA] You've got your children! Are you going to abandon them, in order to remain here with . . . *Nobody!*

DONN'ANNA [*rebelling against this*]: But she'll have another child here! A child whom she may not give to that other man, for it doesn't belong to him!

FRANCESCA [*violently*]: Donn'Anna, aren't you ashamed of what you're saying?

LUCIA: And what about you? Aren't you ashamed of what I'd be doing?

DONN'ANNA [*suddenly crumpling*]: No! No! Your mother is right, my daughter! She has realized that it's for my own sake that I've been saying what I've said. Not for the sake of the child. Now I too am becoming wretched, utterly wretched! But it's because . . . Because now *I* am dying. You see? Yes . . . The moment the child you bear is born to you . . . Far, far away . . . The moment you give him life . . . The *new* life . . . Life outside your body . . . You see? Then you will be the mother! And I shall be the mother no longer! No one will ever come back here again to seek me out! It's all over for me! In that child whom you shall deliver into life you will have . . . *Him! My son!* . . . A little boy . . . Just like him . . . Mine . . . With his golden hair . . . And his smiling eyes . . . Just like him. He'll be yours, and mine no longer! You, you will be the mother! I shall no longer be the mother! And now . . . At this moment . . . Now I am dying, truly dying! Oh, God! Oh, God! [*And she weeps. She weeps as she has never wept before. The others are dismayed; the hearts of the other mother and of her daughter are torn by the compassion they feel for her. Little by little the violence of her weeping subsides. Her voice becomes increasingly dull and colourless, till at last it is all but extinguished.*] Yes! Yes! I must weep no more! No more! If it's for myself that I'm weeping, then . . . No! No! I don't want to weep! I won't! I have wept enough! [*There is a very long pause. Then she gets up, goes over to* LUCIA *and caresses her.*] You must go, my daughter! Go! Go out into your life! So that you too may be consumed! You too are but poor suffering flesh and blood. For that, that is the real meaning of death. And that's enough on that subject. Don't let's think about it any more. Rather . . . Yes, let's . . . Let's think about your mother now. She must be feeling tired.

FRANCESCA: No! No! The one thing I want to do is to leave this house! And immediately! This very moment!

DONN'ANNA: Ah, I'm afraid that's impossible! You can't leave immediately, Mrs Noretti. You'll have to wait. The train for Pisa goes through here rather late in the day. You'll have plenty of time to have a good rest. Plenty of time. And you, my daughter . . .

LUCIA: No! No! I'm not going! I won't go! I'm going to stay here with you!

139

FRANCESCA: You're coming with me! She herself has told you you must!

DONN'ANNA: There's no longer anything for you here.

FRANCESCA: And your children are waiting for you! You must make haste!

LUCIA: But I'm not going back! I'm not going back to *him*! You must realize that! It's no longer possible for me to go back! I can't! *I can't and I won't!* How *can* you want me to go back ... *Now?*

DONN'ANNA: And what about me? ... Left here ... Yes, that is the real meaning of death, my daughter ... So many things that have to be done ... Whether we feel like doing them or not. So many things that have to be said ... And now ... Now we must look up the timetable. Then there'll be the cab to the station ... Travelling ... For we are the dead who are poor and busy ... To embrace martyrdom, to seek consolation, and to achieve peace ... Yes, that is the real meaning of ... *Death.*

LAZARUS

Lazzaro

TRANSLATED BY FREDERICK MAY

For permission to perform this play apply to the International Copyright Bureau, 26 Charing Cross Road, London WC2. For the right to use this translation apply to J. van Loewen Ltd., 81/83 Shaftesbury Avenue, London W1.

Lazarus is unique among Pirandello's plays in having had its world première in England. Translated by C. K. Scott-Moncrieff, it was first presented at the Theatre Royal, Huddersfield, 8 July 1929, by the late Alfred Wareing, with the following cast:

DIEGO SPINA	*Donald Wolfit*
SARA	*Edith Sharpe*
LUCIO	*André Van Gyseghem*
LIA	*May Collie*
ARCADIPANE	*Arthur R. Whatmore*
MONSIGNOR LELLI	*Brian Oulton*
MARRA	*Rodney Millington*
DEODATA	*E. Laura Webster*
GIONNI	*Alan Wheatley*
CICO	*Charles Lefeaux*
A DOCTOR	*Philip Booth*

Produced by Arthur R. Whatmore

Frederick May's version of *Lazarus* was first presented by the Italian Society of the University of Leeds in the Riley-Smith Theatre, 5 December 1955, with the following cast:

DIEGO SPINA	*Gordon Pavey*
SARA	*Gillian Costin*
LUCIO	*Malcolm McKernan*
LIA	*June Shaw*
ARCADIPANE	*John Brewster*
MONSIGNOR LELLI	*Derek Boughton*
MARRA	*George Campbell*
DEODATA	*Norma Clarkson*
GIONNI	*Brian Taylor*
CICO	*George Blenkinsop*
A DOCTOR	*Alan Sommers*

Produced by Derek Boughton

CHARACTERS

DIEGO SPINA

SARA, his wife, but now no longer living with him

LUCIO and LIA, their children

ARCADIPANE, a farm-bailiff

DEODATA, Lia's governess

GIONNI, a doctor of medicine engaged in research

MONSIGNOR LELLI

CICO, God's rent-collector

MARRA, a notary

THE TWO NATURAL CHILDREN of Sara and
    Arcadipane (they do not speak)

A DOCTOR

A POLICEMAN

PEOPLE WHO COME IN FROM THE STREET

TWO PEASANTS

The time is the present (i.e. 1929)

ACT ONE

The scene is the hanging garden at the house of DIEGO SPINA. *The house, an old and unpretentious building, is on the Left (the actor's Left, that is). The front wall is seen in profile; there is a small drooping rustic porch, supported by pillars, beneath which one can see the doors that lead into the rooms on the ground floor. Along the back of the stage there runs a wall between three and four feet high, roughly constructed, whitewashed and topped off with a crest of broken glass. Half-way along this wall, and sharply outlined against the background of the strange blue sky – it's almost as if it were enamelled – there is a huge black cross bearing a depressing, painted, bleeding figure of Christ. Beside the cross there rises the trunk of a very tall cypress tree, which grows up from the road that lies below the wall. This wall, which bounds the house, continues round the Right-hand side of the stage; it is broken into mid-way along by the upper landing of the flight of steps leading down to the road. At ground-level there are one or two flower-beds, with flowering plants here and there, intersected by gravel paths on which stand some seats painted green.*

[*When the curtain rises* DEODATA *and* LIA *are on stage.* LIA *is fifteen, but looks a mere child. Her hair falls loosely over her shoulders, and is set off by a lovely bow of sky-blue ribbon. Her legs are paralysed, and she is confined to an invalid-chair which she wheels about herself with a speed and dexterity that have become second nature to her. Her legs are covered by a shawl.* DEODATA *is about forty. Tall and strongly-built, she is dressed in black and is wearing a black cap on her head. She is seated on an iron stool and is making lace on a pillow. It is an April afternoon.*]

LIA [*absorbedly*]: He hasn't written for more than a month.

DEODATA [*after a pause*]: Lucio?

LIA: And his last letter . . . Well, Daddy couldn't make head or tail of it. He wouldn't let me read it.

DEODATA: He's probably all worked up about his exams. Your father, as usual, is busy getting all sorts of wrong ideas into his head.

LIA: Maybe. But I'm just as bad, you know. I get ideas like that too.

DEODATA: Good girl! You're just as bad. You've infected me too with this *disease* of yours . . .

LIA: Ugh! No, you mustn't call it a disease . . .

DEODATA: Yes, it's a *disease*! A disease! Because . . . Oh, time and time again you . . . Look! You start imagining that somebody's thinking something. You make that person aware of what you're imagining. And the thought that didn't in the first place exist at all, now really does come into his head. And who has made that thought come into his head? *You* . . . By imagining what you did.

LIA: Forgive me for asking, but aren't *you* busy doing a little imagining at the moment? Suggesting that Lucio doesn't write because he's worried about his exams?

DEODATA: I'm just trying to find some sort of an explanation for his silence. Like many another explanation, it might quite well be the probable one. And it's got the virtue too of being one that, while I'm busy imagining it, doesn't harm him and doesn't cause me to grieve . . . At least, not till I have to. [*There is a pause.*]

LIA: Oh, if only he hadn't been so obstinate about going up to the university!

DEODATA: Ah, as for that . . . You see, I didn't approve of him going there either. When he came out of the seminary he could have settled down quietly and contentedly and followed his sacred calling as a priest, without going off to learn all that devilry they teach you up there at the university!

LIA: But if he'd done that he'd have had to go off immediately and do his military service . . .

DEODATA: Oh yes, I know that! That was his excuse for doing what he did. As if he wasn't going to have to do it just the same when he was twenty-six! If you want my opinion, he'd have found it much less of a burden at twenty-one! But there, what's the use of talking about it? Your father too ... The thought of seeing him turn up at any minute without his cassock, and in a soldier's uniform ... Well, for *him*, it would have been like seeing the Devil himself!

LIA: It was because Lucio was so run-down. He couldn't bear the thought of his having to face all the rough and tumble of life in the army ...

DEODATA: It's no use! In this house I shall just have to keep my mouth shut quite tight! I reason things out. I've got into the nasty, vicious habit of reasoning things out, living here among you people ...

LIA: Who don't reason anything out at all ...

DEODATA: Now listen! There's no happy medium about this family! Either you're mad or you're saints. Your father's probably a saint ... No, he certainly *is* a saint! But sometimes, you know, if I forget myself and really start paying attention to what he's doing and saying, well ... God forgive me! ... But ... With those glaring eyes of his ... He really and truly seems to me to be stark staring mad!

LIA [*she smiles her amusement*]: Why don't you tell him so?

DEODATA: I shall, don't you worry! I'll tell him all right! I've been bottling it up inside me for a long time now! I'll tell him this very day, in front of everybody! It'll help to get it off my conscience too! You make me laugh, you and your 'run-down'! Why is he run-down? Because of the life he led in the seminary! Too shut up! Too much hard studying! If you want my opinion, the remedy for all his troubles was a complete change. A life in the open-air! But, oh no! Not on your life! On with his studies! Heaven only knows how long he's going to go on cramming stuff into

that head of his! He'll end up by completely ruining his
health! But when you've told him all this and *shown* him
what it all adds up to . . . It means absolutely nothing as far
as he's concerned. He bothers about people's health as little
as he bothers about anything else! He spreads out his hands
and raises his eyes to Heaven. Or if you do think that he's
been listening to what you've been saying, and that he's
picked up some suggestion that you've let fall, all of a
sudden you're brought up against the realization that what
you suggested . . . Well, he's simply made use of it to com-
mit some fresh piece of lunacy. Like what he's up to now . . .

LIA: You mean handing over the farm?

DEODATA: Yes. A fine way of giving you country air! Which
is what me and Dr Gionni next door suggested to him!

LIA: But what is it he means to do?

DEODATA: With the farm? D'you mean to say you still
haven't realized? He's turning it into a hospice for the
indigent poor.

LIA: And what does that mean?

DEODATA: It means that all the beggars in town, and for miles
around, will get their board and lodging, here on the farm,
at his expense! And that you two, him and you, will be
living there with them! Yes, *yes!* You'll thrive wonder-
fully on the country air! Oh yes, you mark my words!
You'll thrive on it all right! After it's been thoroughly
polluted by all their wretched filthy rags and tatters!

[CICO'S *voice is heard coming from the foot of the steps
Right.*]

CICO'S VOICE: May I come up? Any objections?

DEODATA: Oh, it's you, Cico? Come on up! Come on!

[CICO *comes up the steps. He is a queer little wisp of an old
man. His eyes are small and blue – almost glassy – sharp,
merry, eloquent. On his scalp, which gleams with a high polish,
he is wearing a small red convict's cap. Twisted round his neck
is a long blue scarf, which hangs down before and behind. He*

*speaks in spasmodic outbursts: every now and again he breaks
off short, and looks at you with those small, merry, eloquent
eyes of his, accompanying his gaze with a mute smile, instinct
with shrewdness and cunning.*]

CICO: Ruined, Deodata, ruined. [*He sees* LIA *and immediately
he whips off his cap.*] Ah, so you're here too, dear little lady?
Your humble servant! [*Then once more to* DEODATA]
Ruined.

DEODATA: Who's ruined you, you stupid old donkey?

LIA: Daddy, I'll bet!

CICO: *And the Devil!* Daddy and the Devil! The pair of them.
That's how things happen, little lady. The more a man's a
saint, the closer the Devil creeps up to his elbow. [*Sneezes.*]
Do you mind? [*He puts his cap on again.*] Once I start sneez-
ing . . . Which God forbid! . . . I'm quite capable of letting
rip with a hundred blasts one straight after the other! And
it's good-bye to what I was saying! I can't get another word
out!

LIA: What have they done to you, Daddy and the Devil?

CICO: I've told you . . . *Ruined me!* I'd got a wonderful idea!
Oh, it was a wonderful idea! I was raking the money in in
sackfuls. I'd discovered a profession for myself. I'd taken
out my licence.

DEODATA: You mean you'd given up begging?

CICO: Begging my foot! *I* am a rent collector. Licensed.

DEODATA: You, a rent collector?

LIA: For whom?

CICO: For God, little lady. God's rent-collector. I'd composed
a bit of patter, and as soon as I began to recite it . . . Oh,
you can't imagine the huge crowds I had gathering all
round me!

Men and women, of every class, age
and profession –
sailors, countryfolk, townsfolk –

we are all tenants
of The Lord.

Tenants of The Lord,
Who is the Owner of two houses.

Two houses . . .
Yes . . .
Two houses.

One of them . . . Look, we can see it . . . Look, look at it
    . . . All around us.
And The Lord would be a good and kindly Landlord
to all of us alike,
if it wasn't for the fact that so many, so many of us,
avid in greed and haughty in their pride,
had taken it as their own private property,
when it
ought instead to be a house common to us all.
There's some that've got granaries, barns, and storelofts;
and there's some that haven't got a yard of rope
nor enough wall to stick a nail in,
so as to be able to hang themselves;
and it's most of us that're like this, and that're like me.
But meanwhile the others had better be thinking
that God's the Landlord
of the other house as well . . . The one up there,
the one He makes us pay the rent for
. . . Each and every one of us . . .
In advance, whilst we're still down here.
The poor, like me,
we pay it every day with the suffering
and the toil we know, punctually, at every hour of the
    night and day;
as far as the rich are concerned, on the other hand, all
    that's asked of them by way of payment
is to do the odd good turn every now and again.

And so it comes about,
ladies and gentlemen, that I'm really and truly
here in The Lord's Name
to claim, [*He holds out his hand*]
the little something that's due
from you.
God's rent-collector – that's me!

The money came raining in, little lady. Like hailstones. But now, with all this devilry of a hospice that your father's thinking of founding . . . Well, you can imagine just how much rent in advance for the house up there I'm likely to collect from now on! They'll all say to me, 'You've now got a house yourself down here . . . Go and live in it!'

DEODATA: Good for you, Cico! So you too think this idea of the hospice is the suggestion of the Devil? Eh?

CICO: Of course it is! And I've got the proof of it tucked away inside me! D'you know what I've got inside me?

LIA: Yes, I do. Yes. It's the Devil that says 'No'.

CICO: You're right . . . I swear he does too! He's always doing it! Without me wanting him to! I say 'Yes', and he says 'No'. And he says it in my own voice. In a whisper . . . Right down low . . . While I'm speaking. Look, here's what I mean . . . Yesterday, I was standing in front of a mirror stuck in a shop-window. I said to myself, 'Why, God, *why*? You've given us teeth, and one by one You take them away from us. You've given us sight, and You take it away from us. You've given us strength, and You take it away from us. Now look at me, Lord, look at the state You've left me in! Just look at me! So, of all the lovely things You've given us, we aren't supposed to bring any of them back to You when we come? I must say You'll enjoy Yourself a hundred years from now, when You see a bunch of scarecrows like me popping up in front of You!'

DEODATA: That was the Devil talking! It couldn't possibly have been you!

CICO: Oh, it wasn't! *Positively* it wasn't! It was the Devil. And I was ever so glad that Monsignor Lelli, who happened to be passing at the time, gave him the reply he was asking for! 'Oh, you stupid stupid donkey, God has brought you to this condition so that it shall not trouble you greatly to die!'

DEODATA: And quite right too! Good for Monsignor Lelli!

CICO: As you say! But do you know what that stinking Devil actually dared to fling back at him in a whisper? Right down low he whispered it! 'Then when He takes away our teeth He ought to take away our desire to chew as well . . . And He *doesn't*!' Oh, they all burst out laughing – Monsignor Lelli along with the rest of them. And I was left there, looking a proper muggins, I can tell you! It wasn't right . . . It wasn't fair of them to laugh! Leaving me like that, without a word to say for myself by way of reply! It's not the sort of thing people *ought* to find funny! This what-I've-said about the hospice . . . This charity home . . . That was one of the things he's been telling me . . . Deep down inside me.

DEODATA: The Devil, you mean?

CICO: The Devil. Every time I got to the end of my bit of patter he'd say, 'But, in the meantime, what about if the poor had a house of their own down here as well?' D'you understand? And now the Master's really and truly gone and given them one! [*The voice of* DR GIONNI *is heard as he climbs the steps.*]

DR GIONNI'S VOICE: She's alive again! She's alive again! [*And* DR GIONNI *comes into sight. He is carrying a small white doe-rabbit in his hands. He hurries over to* LIA's *chair. He's a handsome, unattractive man, with a full fair beard, gold-rimmed spectacles . . . About forty years of age. He is wearing a long white linen operating-theatre gown, belted in the middle.*]

GIONNI: Here you are! Here's your dear little rabbit for you again! She's come back to life.

LIA [*quivering all over with a joy which is almost dismay, she takes the rabbit*]: Alive? Oh, dear! Yes! Yes! Look!

DEODATA: Is it possible?

GIONNI: Since last night, as a matter of fact. Yes, soon after I took her home with me . . .

LIA: Oh, so very soon?

GIONNI: I didn't say a word to you about it this morning, because I wanted to be quite sure first . . .

LIA: But what have you done to her? How did you do it?

GIONNI: Nothing. Just a little prick with a needle.

LIA: Oh, my poor little Riri! Where?

GIONNI: In her heart.

LIA [*utterly astonished*]: In her heart? And she came back to life again?

GIONNI: She's not the first case.

DEODATA: Get along with you! Who are you trying to fool? It's a different rabbit!

GIONNI [*to* LIA]: Do *you* think it's a different rabbit?

LIA: Why, of course I don't! It's Riri! [*To* DEODATA] Do you really think I don't know her? Look, she knows me too!

CICO: Oh, no! No! This just can't be! She was dead . . . And you've brought her back to life?

DEODATA: It's a different rabbit, I tell you! Or if it's the same one . . . Well, that means it wasn't dead in the first place!

LIA: She was as dead as dead could be!

GIONNI: Adrenalin.

LIA: And now she's alive!

CICO: Oh, I'm going barmy!

[DIEGO SPINA *and* MONSIGNOR LELLI *enter from the steps.* DIEGO SPINA *is a little over forty. Tall and lean, with an intensely pale and cadaverous face, the whole force and expression of which are concentrated in the fierce glow of his hard, ever-mobile eyes. They are the eyes, you might almost* say, of an infuriated madman. His beard and moustache are sparse, straggling, and unkempt. His hair is parted in the middle and piled up on either side of the parting, as a consequence of the habit he has of pushing the masses of hair up like this when he passes his hands over his head. MONSIGNOR LELLI, outwardly sweet and gentle, is not always successful in concealing beneath his smile and his friendly gaze all the bitterness that lurks in his heart. He is very old.]

DIEGO [coming forward]: What's happening?

LIA [immediately; exultant]: Oh, it's you, Daddy? Look! Look at my Riri! She's come back to life again!

DIEGO: What on earth are you talking about?

LIA: Look at her! Just look at her! Here she is . . . Alive!

DIEGO: It's not possible!

CICO [to MONSIGNOR LELLI]: Dead, and he's brought her back to life again!

MONSIGNOR LELLI [with the smile of a man who doesn't believe what he's saying]: A miracle?

CICO [quivering with rage]: Tell him at once that it's nothing of the sort! Don't laugh! It's not right, Monsignor, it's not proper!

MONSIGNOR LELLI: I'm not laughing, Cico! But, forgive me, if the rabbit has contrived to come back to life . . .

DIEGO [promptly, harshly]: It's a sure sign that it can't possibly have been dead in the first place!

MONSIGNOR LELLI: Obviously! All quite simple!

DEODATA: There, just what I said myself!

LIA: No, Daddy! She was dead! She was really and truly dead! Wasn't she, Doctor?

DIEGO [peremptory, stern, clipping his words incisively, without giving the DOCTOR a chance to reply]: It cannot possibly be true! [Then, turning once more to the DOCTOR, with an air of nervous irritation] Really, Doctor, you oughtn't to . . . You ought not to . . .

GIONNI [as though unable to understand why all this fuss is being *made about something which, to him, is the most natural thing in the world*]: What oughtn't I to do?

DIEGO: You oughtn't to tell my daughter such abominable stories!

GIONNI: Why do you call them abominable?

DIEGO: Oh, so you think it's quite normal for us to be able to . . . ?

GIONNI: If you'd only taken the trouble to keep up with . . .

DIEGO: I have done so! We can read all about them in the newspapers, unfortunately, these triumphs of science – and all the other things like them! And I know all about the disgraceful way you torture those wretched little animals you keep in your laboratory! It appals me, *utterly*.

GIONNI: But I've brought this one back to life . . .

MONSIGNOR LELLI [*instantly*]: . . . from what was *apparently* death.

GIONNI [*promptly and firmly*]: There was no *apparently* about it at all. She *was* dead.

DIEGO: Do you mind telling me how you can be so dogmatic about it.

GIONNI: Good Lord, do you really suppose that a doctor doesn't know when . . . ?

DIEGO [*severely, cutting him off short*]: I know this . . . God alone can, by means of a miracle, recall the dead to life.

CICO: There you are! Good for you!

MONSIGNOR LELLI: Precisely!

GIONNI: That, Monsignor, is my belief too. God alone. I do not for one moment presume to have wrought the miracle myself. I can, you see, conceive of science as another instrument apt to the Hand of God. Everything depends upon our being able to comprehend one another.

MONSIGNOR LELLI: Are you really serious? I mean . . . About the way *you* interpret what's happened.

GIONNI: As serious as I'm convinced of the truth of our faith . . . Yours and mine.

DIEGO [*angrily, contemptuously, he snatches the rabbit out of* LIA'*s hands and gives it to* GIONNI]: Here, take it! Take it back to your laboratory!

LIA [*impulsively*]: No, not my Riri!

DIEGO: That will do, Lia!

GIONNI: My intention, Mr Spina, was to bring a little joy to your daughter. Is this how you thank me?

MONSIGNOR LELLI: There is one faith, and one faith only!

GIONNI: And that bids me take this rabbit back to my laboratory?

LIA: No, Daddy!

MONSIGNOR LELLI [*to* LIA]: If God took her from you . . .

GIONNI: God is giving her back to her again!

DIEGO [*at the end of his tether*]: Doctor, I beg you, will you please . . . ? Really!

GIONNI: Very well, then! I'll take her back with me! I'll take her! [*He goes off towards the steps. Just before he begins his descent he turns to* LIA] Don't worry, my dear! I'll keep her alive for you!

DIEGO [*lovingly he bends over his weeping daughter*]: I don't like to see you crying . . . I don't want you to cry, Lia . . You know what it is we have to do . . . We offer up to God . . .

LIA: Yes, Daddy . . . Yes! Yes! . . . I'm going in now! I'm going in . . . [*She goes off towards the house in her wheel-chair and disappears through one of the doors under the portico. They all follow her with their eyes.*]

MONSIGNOR LELLI: You might perhaps have let her keep it.

DEODATA [*angry and upset*]: I should just think you might have! An innocent pleasure like that . . . !

MONSIGNOR LELLI: Ah, no! That's the precise point at issue! *Not* innocent! Not when it was regained by such means!

DIEGO [*a touch repentant*]: You heard her say, all of you, didn't you, that as far as she was concerned the creature *was* dead?

DEODATA: And to get it back again . . . Alive . . .

DIEGO [*turning upon her angrily*]: Do you realize the full implications of what you're saying?

CICO: Dead and then back to life again!

DIEGO: That we should believe such a thing possible . . . Do you realize that? And that she should have the proof there on her knees? Oh, I felt so angry deep down inside me . . .

DEODATA: What? Who made you feel angry? The child?

DIEGO: No, listening to that man and what he had to say!

DEODATA: And what had that got to do with the child anyway? Snatching the rabbit out of her hands like that . . . Like a brute . . .

DIEGO: And aren't I confessing that I regret my harshness? It seems to me that I am.

DEODATA: It never entered her head for a single instant to think of any of the horrible things you saw in the affair! Now, you listen to me! I've kept it bottled up long enough! And now I'm going to tell you, here and now, in front of Monsignor Lelli. The trials that God sends us . . . Let's accept them with resignation . . . Well and good! All the sacrifices, all of them . . . If it's Him that commands you to make them . . . Well, make them . . . And be happy to do so . . . Well and good. But it's got to be Him . . . Or His Vicar down here on earth! Look here, Monsignor Lelli'll do just as well . . . If it's in His Name that he orders me to do something. But not you! *You*, if you like, *you* can sacrifice *yourself* . . .

DIEGO: I . . .

DEODATA: Yes, you've been sacrificing yourself, your whole life long! But when you start insisting that other people ought to sacrifice themselves as well . . . Oh no, that's going too far!

DIEGO: I? I start insisting . . . ? Against their will?

DEODATA: That's how I see it anyway! Will . . . What sort of will do you think your daughter's got, when it comes to facing up to you? Yes, I tell you! *Yes!* You sacrifice everyone else along with yourself! Perhaps you don't even notice you're doing it. But look here . . . At this very moment . . . What you're planning to do now . . .

DIEGO: What I'm planning to do?

DEODATA: Oh, that hospice of yours!

DIEGO: Oh, the hospice! Bringing that up again, are you?

DEODATA: Forgive me for asking . . . But have you thought about me? I mean . . . Have you ever given a thought to all the love I've always bestowed on your poor afflicted daughter? All the loving care . . . *My* loving care . . . That now she'll have to go without?

DIEGO: Why will she have to go without it?

DEODATA: You ask me that? You surely don't expect me to come and live in that hospice of yours? Along with all the retired beggars you're pensioning off? I've even heard a rumour that you're going to welcome into your hospice that Scoma slut!

CICO: Yes, Yes! That Scoma woman . . . She goes around telling everybody!

DEODATA: And, of course, we all know why! It's a reward for her virtue!

MONSIGNOR LELLI: That will do, Deodata!

DEODATA [*as though unable to rest in peace, revealing all the resentment of an ancient rivalry*]: That witch! She goes about begging, with her own picture in a frame, slung round her neck like a scapula! And it's not in God's Name that she begs for alms! Oh, no! Oh, no! Not on your life! It's because of what she *was* . . . It's in honour of *that*! And we all know what *she* was, *don't* we? Her picture tells you *that* anyway. You just try not giving her anything! She'll spit the most foul language after you! Curse you up hill and down dale!

MONSIGNOR LELLI: I've already told you, Deodata . . . *That will do!*

DEODATA: Yes, Monsignor, but you do realize, don't you…?

MONSIGNOR LELLI [*his meaning clear, if subtly veiled*]: It would be rather more to the point if you tried to do a little *realizing* yourself!

DEODATA: But I do realize! I do understand! And since you say that . . . Will you allow me to . . . ? No, it's not really me. Will you allow my *conscience* to say a word or two? Don't worry . . . I'll keep quite calm! Calm as calm! It's the voice of conscience. Look deep down inside yourselves. I may be mistaken. But I must speak out frankly. And say all I've got to say. [*To* DIEGO] It's an excuse . . . Nothing more or less . . . An excuse for your own weakness, this idea of yours for founding a hospice up there on the farm!

DIEGO: My *weakness*?

DEODATA: Yes! Your weakness in never having plucked up enough courage to chuck them off the farm . . .

MONSIGNOR LELLI [*with the utmost severity*]: Hold your tongue, Deodata!

DIEGO: No! No! Let her say what she has to say!

DEODATA: *Your wife.* Who's been living there for years and years in mortal sin with a man . . . Your servant . . . Who she's had two children by.

DIEGO [*with a sorrowing simplicity*]: Why do you call it weakness?

DEODATA: 'Why', he says! *Why?* Why, because you've never had the courage to . . .

DIEGO [*promptly, cutting her short*]: I have had the courage to . . . To resist myself! The more what she has done has humiliated me in the esteem of other people, the greater has been the courage I have shown! You're one of those other people yourself! And you call it weakness! Just like the rest of them!

DEODATA: Forgive me for asking, but is this *your* daughter that's here, or isn't it? And tell me . . . Did the doctors prescribe country air for her, or did they not? Even if there wasn't anything else, your daughter . . . Her and her alone

... Your own daughter ought to be able to give you the strength you need, to do what you should have done years ago. Instead of which you keep her shut up here in this house, just so as her mother ... The worthless creature ... Can go on enjoying all the country air herself!

DIEGO [*loudly, so as to cut short what she is saying*]: You're not to talk like that! You don't know what you're talking about!

DEODATA [*after a short pause she says, in a low voice, almost as if she can't help herself, but must say what she has to say – to herself at least*]: So you'll even go so far as to *defend* her!

DIEGO [*promptly, at once*]: No. It's you that're defending her ... Yes, *you*! ... Without knowing that you're doing it.

DEODATA: *I* am?

DIEGO: Yes, *you* are. Because it was she who wanted her daughter to have precisely what you have been demanding for her ... Just now.

DEODATA: Country air?

DIEGO: Country air. [*A pause. Then he says*] Why do you think she left me? We were never able to reach any agreement on how we were to bring up our children. That came first ... Then we disagreed about their education too.

DEODATA: Oh, so that was why she left you?

DIEGO: That was why ... That was why she left me. [*Another short pause.*] Monsignor, she loved them with a love that was ... I don't know ... Too ... In my opinion, too *carnal*. The same as so many other mothers, however ... Neither more nor less.

CICO: Oh, a mother ... [*And immediately he claps his hand over his mouth.*]

DIEGO: And it was on her account, as a matter of fact ... The little girl's ... When she fell ill ... *She* firmly believed that it was all my fault ... Because I'd insisted on sending her away to school too young ... I'd sent her to board with the Sisters ... It was on account of the little girl that she hated me ... She couldn't bear the sight of me any longer

... She cursed my house and went away to live on the farm ...

DEODATA: With that man?

DIEGO [*angrily*]: What do you mean, 'with that man'? That happened two years later. She went to live on the farm ... Waiting for me to take the child out there to her ... The child who by this time had lost the use of her legs.

DEODATA: Ah! ... And you ... ?

DIEGO: I refused.

DEODATA: That was wrong of you!

DIEGO [*to* MONSIGNOR LELLI]: She made it a condition of our reconciliation that I should fetch the other child back home as well.

DEODATA: Lucio?

DIEGO: Lucio. She wanted me to remove him from the seminary to which I'd sent him. Monsignor, I might ... Perhaps ... Have done that even. But to admit that it was all my fault ...

MONSIGNOR LELLI: You mean, what happened to the little girl?

DIEGO: In all conscience I couldn't bring myself to believe that it was my fault! And if I'd withdrawn Lucio ... Prevented him from following his career in the Church ... As if by way of making amends for the fault into which I'd fallen ... If I'd done this, it would have led to my doing with my children ... From that day forth ... Just exactly whatever *she* decided ...

MONSIGNOR LELLI: Inevitably.

DIEGO: It would have meant being false to myself, to what I felt to be true, to my principles ...

MONSIGNOR LELLI: And you say that you might even have done all this?

DIEGO: Yes. I was on the point of doing it ... More than once.

MONSIGNOR LELLI: It grieves me to hear you say so!

DIEGO: By the Grace of God, I was able to realize ... Each

time . . . That I should have been doing it because I still loved and . . . *Wanted* that woman . . .

MONSIGNOR LELLI: You see?

DIEGO: And that it was only because of this vile lusting of my flesh . . .

MONSIGNOR LELLI: Yes! You see? You see?

DIEGO: I won the battle with myself. And nobody ever knew the tears I shed as I refused to surrender! And nobody ever knew of my secret hope that *she* might give way instead . . . Out of compassion for her crippled child.

DEODATA: She certainly ought to have felt compassion all right!

DIEGO: The hatred she felt for me was stronger; and she didn't yield.

DEODATA [*with an outburst of diabolical glee*]: You're still in love with her! You're still in love with her!

DIEGO: Of course I'm not! What on earth are you talking about?

DEODATA: It's as plain as the nose on your face! You're still in love with her! You can see it a mile off!

CICO [*trembling all over with excitement*]: There you are, you see! It's the Devil again! Mine was just about to say the same thing . . . And hers got his spoke in first!

DIEGO [*with a sad smile*]: Yes, Cico . . . You're quite right . . . It was the Devil. What harm do you think there can possibly be now in this love which I must feel . . . Yes, even for her? I'm right, aren't I, Monsignor? [*To* DEODATA, *after a pause*] As you can see very clearly, it would be unjust of me . . . It would be a double injustice on my part . . . If I were now to take advantage of the fact that Lia needs the country air on account of her health . . . That's to say, of the very remedy which she herself proposed at that time for the child . . . And on account of which . . . Since I refused to give in . . . She is now living in sin.

DEODATA: You don't mean to say, do you now, that you believe that *that's* your fault?

DIEGO: If I had only taken the children up there to her . . .

MONSIGNOR LELLI: No! No! The wrong which you committed was something quite different . . . Something quite, quite different. You did wrong in not throwing her out in time . . . I mean, the moment you saw that she'd taken up with that man . . .

DIEGO: Yes, but . . .

MONSIGNOR LELLI: You ought not to have tolerated it. You ought not to have allowed her go on living her adulterous life in your house . . . If the farm was yours . . . I was under the impression that it belonged to her . . .

DIEGO: No, it's mine. It belongs to me . . .

MONSIGNOR LELLI: It really has been most shocking . . . Perfectly outrageous! But since you didn't do it at the proper time . . . When you had every right to do it . . . Well, you certainly can't do it now. [*To* DEODATA] He can't plead the excuse of his daughter's health . . . Not now. That would put him in the wrong and her in the right.

DIEGO: No . . . You see, Monsignor, you don't know what a terrible effect it had on me when first I heard of it! What I saw myself as on the very brink of doing in the first blind impulse! Keeping myself in check . . . Doing nothing . . . Just like that! . . . Living out the life of my torment . . . Letting it go on and on . . . Without affording it the slightest relief . . . Quite the reverse in fact . . . I chose rather to be the scorn of all my neighbours . . . The button which is radiant in the fire that moulds it . . . That was my victory . . . *Martyrdom.* A long, long martyrdom. It was long because my wound kept on opening afresh . . . And the blood . . . Black, *bitter* blood . . . Welled out again and again. They told me that she'd given up everything . . . That she'd cast off all her lovely clothes . . .

DEODATA: Ah, but that's because she knows that . . . Well, dressing the way she does now . . .

DIEGO: Like a peasant, you mean?

DEODATA: Yes . . . She's an absolute joy to look at . . . So lovely . . . Everybody says the same thing . . . An absolute delight . . .

CICO: Oh yes, she's lovely . . . Lovely! She still looks like a girl of twenty! When she passes by everybody turns to look at her. It's just as if the sun was passing by! She's a *miracle*!

DEODATA [*she is alluding to* SARA'*s bailiff lover*]: I suppose she looks so lovely, because that's how *he* wants her!

DIEGO [*with a sudden, extremely violent access of rage, which dismays and chills them all*]: That will be enough on *that* subject! I can't bear to stand here and listen to . . . *Not from you!*

DEODATA [*dully, insensitively, after a pause*]: It was you who brought the subject up in the first place . . .

DIEGO: It wasn't out of wickedness that she gave herself to that man. Neither is he the sort of man that you're supposing. You know, Monsignor, don't you, that he's always sent the profits on the farm to the hospital? All of them. In my name. Ever since I first refused to accept them. And those profits have gone on steadily increasing, year by year. That farm has become the richest and the best cultivated in the whole neighbourhood.

CICO: Oh, it's Paradise itself! An Earthly Paradise! I go out there, so I know! And those two little boys . . . They're more handsome even than their mother! And they're already working on the land. Oh, you should just see them! Hoeing away, with two little hoes . . . *So* big! . . . Working away beside their father . . . And simply bursting with health!

DIEGO: It would certainly be a very great pity to turn them out . . . A pity for the hospital, I mean.

DEODATA: Well, I'm . . . ! He's thinking of the hospital now!

DIEGO: What I'm thinking is that they live there as poor people . . . Doing good to others. If I turn them out now, they'll have to provide for themselves . . .

DEODATA: It'll be their punishment!

DIEGO: That's as may be! But the good that they've been doing all this time mustn't just be allowed to go to waste. I shall have to carry on the good work they've been doing myself . . .

DEODATA: By setting up your hospice on the farm? You'll ruin the farm! And as for the amount of good you'll be able to do . . . ! That'll be precious little! And, what's more, you've done as much good as you need to already! It's high time you stopped! You've stripped yourself of everything! As a matter of fact, it was about this point that I wanted to talk to you, Monsignor . . . Has he got the right to carry on the way he does? When he's got a daughter who's a cripple?

DIEGO: My daughter wants for nothing . . . Save only to attain in Heaven . . . When it shall please God to call her unto Him . . . All that here on earth she could not have. It's not enough to *talk* about poverty . . . We must *experience* it. And, since that's the case, we must strip ourselves of all that we possess. My daughter will live in the country, but she will see there . . . A poor man among other poor men . . . Her own father. And she will be happy, because she will see that *I* am happy! Yes, when all's said and done, that is the only way! Otherwise I couldn't possibly bear to think of those two, driven off the land, and wanderers on the face of the earth, in search of work. [*Turning abruptly to* DEODATA] Don't stand there staring at me like that! I pray every night to God that He will call me back unto Himself! Not that I may have relief from the trials which He has been pleased to visit upon me, but that I may raise *them* up from that life of sin which is now theirs. Because I know that she has found a man . . . She has found a man.

[*During his speech the sun has been setting, and now the sky is all aflame with the full splendour of sunset. A bell is heard ringing at the foot of the steps.*]

DEODATA: Somebody's ringing. Wonder who it can be? The gate ought to be open, unless *you* shut it when you came in. [*To* CICO] Go and see who it is, will you? Go on! [CICO *goes over to the steps. He starts back in utter astonishment, almost in dismay. He comes back over.*]

CICO: Ooooh! It's *her*! Her! The Missis!

DIEGO: She's . . . *Here*?

CICO: Yes . . . All dressed in red . . . With a black cloak.

DEODATA: She must have got to hear about the . . . And perhaps she's come to . . .

MONSIGNOR LELLI: About the farm?

DIEGO: But how does she dare to . . . ?

MONSIGNOR LELLI [*catches sight of her as she appears on the steps and halts on the landing*]: Here she comes!

DIEGO [*in a low voice*]: Go indoors, all of you. Leave me alone with her. [*To* DEODATA] Mind that Lia doesn't find out she's here.

[MONSIGNOR LELLI, DEODATA, and CICO *withdraw. They go out through one of the doors under the portico. Set against the background of the blazing sky* SARA, *dressed all in red under a black cloak, seems like an unreal apparition of ineffable beauty: she radiates freshness, health, and power.*]

SARA [*absorbed by what she sees, she looks around her, comparing her memory of things with how they appear to her now – less ample, meaner, shabbier*]: The garden . . . The house . . .

DIEGO: You actually dare to come and see me again? In front of the whole world?

SARA [*the same absorbed, appraising look*]: And you too . . . My God, what a face!

DIEGO: Leave my face out of this! Tell me why you've come!

SARA: Oh, don't get worried! As soon as people get to know why I've come, they'll realize that I *had* to come . . . And they won't be at all surprised. There will be a great deal else for them to be surprised about . . . But not my coming here.

DIEGO: Have you come because you've heard . . . ?

SARA: About the hospice? No. [*She laughs.*] Oh, you were afraid that I'd come to intercede, to beg you to leave us on the farm?

DIEGO: *Isn't* that what you've come for?

SARA: No, no, of course not! It's not your farm that's keeping us alive . . .

DIEGO [*swiftly, trying to cut her short*]: I know! I know!

SARA: Well, then? We live by the work that we do upon it, and that tomorrow we can do somewhere else. It's something that, so far as we're concerned, isn't of the slightest importance. It might, at most . . . Yes, at most . . . It might be of some importance to the poor, sick people at the hospital.

DIEGO: That's the very thing I was saying myself, only a moment or so ago . . .

SARA: Well, you see then? And since you've mentioned the subject . . . Though it's something altogether different I've come here to talk to you about, and I hadn't thought that in coming here I'd have to talk to you about this at all . . . But since you've brought up the subject . . .

DIEGO: No! Tell me first the reason why you've come . . .

SARA: Wait a minute . . . If you're trying to find some excuse for turning us out . . .

DIEGO: It's not an excuse!

SARA: What on earth do you think they want with a farm? . . . These old townee beggars, that are used to spending their lives in wandering from door to door. Used to being with lots of people. If you shut them up up there, they'll feel just as if they were in prison, . . . Being punished – not being done a kindness. In a year's time the farm will have died on their hands.

DIEGO: I shall be up there myself, living among them.

SARA: You? And what could you possibly do with those arms of yours? You make me laugh! You've not seen the farm . . . Not since . . . And you've got no idea what it's like now, no conception of what we've done to it. There's not one square foot of land that's not growing something . . .

DIEGO: I know that . . .

SARA: The kitchen garden . . . The vineyard . . . The orchard . . . Oh, we've got every kind of fruit you could possibly want! And, you know, we've found water! That spring which you said . . . Do you remember? . . . Said you could sometimes hear running under the bank alongside the path that leads down into the valley . . . Well, that's the one . . . We've found it! There's masses and masses of water! It's brought new life and freshness to everything! Three great cisterns always full . . . And it flows along the ditches . . . Everywhere . . . Joyously! And it makes you heave a deep sigh of contentment when you hear its noisy rush on those hot summer evenings when . . . So . . . Listen! . . . If this hospice of yours *is* only an excuse . . . Don't spare the matter another moment's thought.

DIEGO: I've already told you . . . It's not an excuse.

SARA: We'll leave the farm. We'll go away of our own accord. Tomorrow, if you like. We won't even put you to the trouble of turning us out. Put in another bailiff, though . . . Choose an honest one. And a man who knows the meaning of work. That's what you must do. And do it . . . Now, listen to me . . . Do it for the sake of your own flesh and blood! Have you given a thought to how you're going to provide for these children of yours?

DIEGO: The children . . . Do you mean to tell me that you're interested in them . . . *Still?*

SARA: '*Still*', you say? To *me*? *You?* Who was it that denied me the right to think of them *always*? *Always!* Of them and of them alone?

DIEGO [*his face darkening*]: Let's drop the subject!

SARA: You no longer wanted me to be a mother to my children, even though your decision meant that you would lose me as a wife!

DIEGO: Yes, because I intended my wife to be the mother of my children, bringing them up according to my principles.

SARA: Oh, no! No! Not that! Never!

DIEGO: You see, then?

SARA: Do you know what? The fact that things are as they now are proves to me ... More decisively than ever ... That it was I who was right! Not you!

DIEGO: Let's change the subject! Let's change the subject!

SARA [pointing to the Crucifix]: You never see anything but That ... And even That you see only in the way you want to see It.

DIEGO: Don't blaspheme!

SARA: I, blaspheme? I'm the first to go down on my knees before It! But, you know, that Cross is there to give people life ... Not death!

DIEGO: Will you be silent? What right have you to talk of life and death? You have forgotten that the true life is the one which lies in the world beyond. When we have cast off our fleshly habit ...

SARA: I know that God gave us this life as well as that other ... In order that we might live it out, here below, in health and happiness! And no one can know this better than a mother! I wanted joy ... Yes, I wanted joy and health for my children! And I looked for wealth too ... Yes! For their sakes ... Not for my own! I've lived as a peasant myself. I still live as a peasant. And if you leave the farm to your children, then let me tell you ... I shall be glad I've toiled with these arms ... Yes, you know, really and truly toiled! ... To make it as prosperous as it now is ... For their sakes!

DIEGO: They've done without it so far, with the help of God, and they can go on doing without it.

SARA: How can you possibly know that?

DIEGO: I do know.

SARA: So many things may happen of which you haven't the slightest suspicion.

DIEGO: Well anyway, I've provided for one of the children. And as for Lucio . . .

SARA [*as if she had been expecting this*]: As for Lucio . . . ?

DIEGO: He has his vocation.

SARA: And if that is no longer sufficient for him?

DIEGO: What do you mean . . . 'If that is no longer sufficient for him'? It must be sufficient for him!

SARA: Lucio arrived at my house yesterday, and he's been there ever since.

DIEGO [*utterly taken aback*]: Lucio? What on earth are you saying? He's at your . . . ? Where? He's come back . . . ?

SARA: Yes, he's come back. And he came to *me*. That's why I said that the fact that things are as they are proves . . . Now more decisively than ever . . . That I was right.

DIEGO [*still almost incredulous*]: Lucio came to *you*?

SARA: That is why you see me here. Your son came to me.

DIEGO: But . . . What do you mean . . . *Came?* Did you write to him? You sent for him, didn't you?

SARA: How on earth could I possibly have sent for him? No. And why should I have done? [*Scornfully*] Oh, you're still thinking about the farm! As I've told you, I'm ready to hand it over to you tomorrow!

DIEGO: Then . . . It was of his own accord? But . . . Why? [*In dismay and bewilderment*] He came without showing his face here . . . He's stopped writing . . . What's happened to him?

SARA: I don't know. I was in the vegetable garden. I saw him standing before me. I didn't recognize him at first. How on earth *should* I have recognized him?

DIEGO: But . . . He came out to you? With what object? What did he say to you?

SARA: Oh, the things he said to me . . . I can't repeat them to you . . . Not in the way he said them . . . You must hear him say them for yourself!

DIEGO: Things . . . Things that were meant for you?

SARA: No, not for me . . . For the whole wide world!

DIEGO: He must have gone mad!

SARA: No! Nothing of the sort! Mad indeed! He's a changed man!

DIEGO: *A changed man?* What do you mean? He must at least have given you some reason for his coming.

SARA: Yes, he did. It was to recognize me.

DIEGO [*in bewildered astonishment*]: To *recognize* you?

SARA: Yes. And to be born again. *He*, to be born again of me. To be born again of me, his mother. He said so! I looked at him, in dismay. How white his face has grown, just like wax! And his eyes! I saw him stretch out his arms . . . Two tears welled up within those terrible eyes of his . . . 'Mummy!' he said . . . I felt myself . . . I felt myself purified by it . . . A blessèd mother once again! He took me in his arms . . . He wept on my breast . . . For a long time . . . A very long time . . . In my arms . . . Trembling all over. I've never felt anyone tremble the way he did then!

DIEGO [*almost to himself*]: Oh, God! O God, help me! Support me, O God! God, God, what is it that You would with me? [*To* SARA] But . . . How? What . . . ? Without giving a moment's thought to the fact that . . . Up there, where he went to look for you . . . You were living with a man who's not his father . . . And that he . . . [*Suddenly, as though a doubt has entered his mind, leaving him thunderstruck*] But perhaps . . . Oh, God! . . . Perhaps he's no longer wearing his cassock?

SARA: No.

DIEGO [*as if in terror*]: He's taken off his cassock? He's thrown away his cassock?

SARA: But you should hear how lovingly he still speaks of God!

DIEGO [*frantic*]: Where is he? Where is he? Tell me where he is! Is he up at the farm?

SARA: No, he came with me. To talk to you.

DIEGO: He wants to talk to me?

SARA: He wants to explain things to you . . .

DIEGO: Where is he?

SARA: He stayed at my sister's . . . Down by Town Gate . . .

DIEGO: I'm going to see him! I'm going to see him! I'm going to see him . . .

[*And, as if quite insane, he hurls himself down the stairs.* SARA *remains perplexed and a touch dismayed by his flight. She looks around her and perceives* CICO, *who is standing peering at her from behind one of the little columns, red cap on head. She waves him over. Quite suddenly the sky, which up till now has been red, becomes violet, and the stage is as if chilled all at once by this livid, sinister light.*]

SARA: Come over here! Come on! You must run after him! *I* can't. Lucio's come home . . . Without his cassock!

CICO: Oh, has he?

SARA: Yes! Yes! He dashed off like a madman. Go and tell them in the house. Go and tell them in the house. *I'm going now. You must look after him!*

[*And she hurries away down the steps.* DEODATA *comes out of one of the doors of the portico to see what's going on.* CICO *immediately calls out to her.* DEODATA *hastens over.*]

DEODATA: What did she say to you? And why did he run away?

CICO: It's Lucio . . . Lucio . . . It's all the Devil's fault . . . He's thrown away his cassock!

DEODATA: Lucio? Did she tell you that?

CICO: She did! She did! It's all the Devil's fault!

DEODATA: O God, help us! And now what's going to become of that man?

CICO: He tore off, dashed down the stairs! I'm going after him! [*Exit furiously down the stairs.*]

DEODATA: Yes, you go! Run after him! But where will he have gone? Oh, Lord God in Heaven! All dressed in scarlet she was! Like a flame from Hell! And to bring such news too! [*She goes over to the porch*] Oh, Monsignor! Monsignor!

MONSIGNOR LELLI [*coming out, in consternation*]: What's the matter? What's happened?

DEODATA: Lucio's stopped being a priest! He's thrown away his cassock!

MONSIGNOR LELLI: No! What on earth are you saying?

DEODATA: *She* came here ... To break the news to him! And *he's* gone tearing off!

MONSIGNOR LELLI: Where to?

DEODATA: I don't know! He just went dashing off! [*A confused sound of shouting, anxious voices is heard near at hand, and coming even nearer.*]

MONSIGNOR LELLI: Do you hear that? What can have happened? There's a lot of shouting going on!

SHOUTS: Gently, now, gently! ... Up there! ... Up those steps!

But how did it happen?

Oh, it's Mr Spina!

Not so loud! Not so loud! Remember his daughter!

But is he ... *Dead*? How did it happen? Oh, poor soul!

Careful now! Careful as you go up the steps!

Turn round now! Head first! The steps are pretty steep!

DEODATA [*rushing over to the steps*]: Oh, my God! It's the Master! What's happened?

CICO [*coming back up the steps*]: He's been run over! Run over!

MONSIGNOR LELLI: Run along, Deodata! Don't let the child come out!

DEODATA: But he can't be dead!

MONSIGNOR LELLI: No, no! Let's hope not! Now run along! Run along!

[*A group of men comes up the steps, panting. They are men who were passing along the street when the accident occurred. They are supporting the limp body of* DIEGO SPINA, *some at the head, others at the feet. There is also a number of people*

173

carrying small lighted lanterns. Laboriously the men carry the body over and set it down on one of the benches, so that it is in full view of the audience. DEODATA *rushes over towards the house. When the knot of bearers has passed the head of the steps . . . That's to say, before they've got to the point of putting the body down . . . Another group of curious, anxious people comes into sight. Their way is barred by* CICO.]

VOICES OF THE BEARERS: Up a bit! Gently does it! Over here! Over here!

Put him down on that seat there!

That's it! That's the ticket! Gently now! Over here!

MONSIGNOR LELLI: But there's no sign of any injury!

ONE OF THE BEARERS: No, not a sign!

MONSIGNOR LELLI: How did it happen?

ANOTHER OF THE BEARERS: He threw himself under a motor-car!

MONSIGNOR LELLI: What . . . *Deliberately?* Impossible!

FIRST BEARER: Well, it certainly seemed like it!

THIRD BEARER: He was running along just like somebody gone stark staring mad!

FOURTH BEARER: Everybody thought the same thing . . . That he'd . . .

MONSIGNOR LELLI: Impossible! Impossible!

FIRST BEARER: The car swerved . . .

SECOND BEARER: Didn't even go over him . . .

THIRD BEARER: But it flung him against the wall so violently that he dropped down at once . . . Just like a lump of lead!

MONSIGNOR LELLI: He doesn't seem to show any sign of life!

FOURTH BEARER: Doesn't he? He was breathing up till a moment or so ago.

MONSIGNOR LELLI: He's quite cold!

CICO [*from the head of the steps, intent upon clearing a path through the curious bystanders*]: Here's the Doctor! Here comes the Doctor! Mind out of the way there! Mind out of the way!

[*The* DOCTOR *hurries up the steps and across the stage. He
has been summoned in haste from the nearest surgery.*]

DOCTOR [*as he hurries over, to* CICO, *who is trying to tell him all
about it*]: Yes, I know . . . I'd realized that . . . Run over!
Do you mind? Let me get through! . . . Let me have a look
at him!

[*He bends over* SPINA, *studies his appearance for a moment
or so, unbuttons his collar, waistcoat, shirt . . . Listens to his
heart. In the meantime there is low murmur of comment from
the bystanders.*]

BYSTANDERS: Looks as if he's dead!

H'm! Yes!

What a terrible thing to happen!

Hush! Ssssh!

DOCTOR [*raising his head*]: He's dead.

BYSTANDERS [*in various tones of voice*]: Dead?

DOCTOR [*once more he bends down to listen to the injured man's
heart. Then he gets up again, and, amidst the bewilderment and
anguish, the dismay and the compassion felt by all about him,
says*]: Dead.

ACT TWO

The scene is the rustic porch of DIEGO SPINA's *farmhouse in the country. The tiles of the lean-to-style roof, which slopes away towards the back of the stage, are visible from underneath. The roof itself is supported by two pillars which are set in a low outer wall, that is broken into midway along so as to allow of access – effected by means of a short flight of steps – to the porch. A stone bench runs along this wall. In the background you can see the farm: a dazzling, exultant expanse of verdure, resplendent in the sunshine – an earthly paradise. In the right-hand wall of the porch there is the opening for the staircase which leads to the upper floor of the villa. On either side of this opening there is a stone seat set against the wall. Towards the back of the stage, and beyond the stage seat, there is a small door let into the wall. In the wall Left there is the door which opens into the bailiff's quarters. It is up one step. In the middle of the stage there are an old rustic table, some old chairs, and a stool or two.*

[*When the curtain rises* ARCADIPANE *and an old peasant are on stage. The peasant is already laden with one or two bundles, and another bundle is lying on the ground. In addition there's a large saddlebag on the table.* ARCADIPANE *is a tall, powerfully-built man, with a curly black beard; his eyes are large, smiling and as innocent as a child's. He is wearing a shaggy black cap which he has made for himself out of goatskin. He's dressed like a peasant, in blue broadcloth and jackboots. Instead of a waistcoat he's wearing, over his coarse, white linen shirt, another shirt – made from violet flannel, and chequered with red and black squares. The loose, floppy collar of the linen shirt is folded down over that of the flannel shirt. Around his waist he has a leather belt.*]

ARCADIPANE [*picking up the bundle from the ground*]: See if you can carry this one as well. Then we'll have finished . . .

Everything'll be out. [*Carefully and considerately he loads the bundle on to the peasant's back. Meanwhile another peasant comes in through the door Left, carrying a chest painted green.* SARA *follows him in. The bells of an approaching carriage can be heard in the distance.*]

SARA: Is this chest to go on the cart too?

ARCADIPANE: Yes. [*To the peasant*] But wait till I get there before you put it on the cart. I'll come and do it myself. I'll have to find a place to put it. And make sure everything's strapped down properly. Come on, let's be going. I'll take the bag. [*He picks it up.*]

SARA: The bag goes on the mule.

ARCADIPANE: Oh, there's a carriage coming. It can't be them, surely?

SARA: No. It's too soon.

ARCADIPANE: There's nothing more left upstairs?

SARA: Nothing at all. Go and see who it is, will you? But it can't possibly be them.

[*She goes back into the house.* ARCADIPANE *leaves the porch, following the peasants, who have already gone out Back and turned to the Left. For a moment the stage remains empty. Then* ARCADIPANE *re-enters Back, followed by* DR GIONNI.]

ARCADIPANE: Well, here we are! Do come in, Doctor. If you'd like to go upstairs . . . I don't know if that's what you want to do . . . My quarters are over here . . . And the boy's up there . . . [*He points to the staircase Right*].

GIONNI: No. No. I must be on my way again immediately. I'll come back, after I've made my visit. I've got to see a neighbour of yours. Over at Lotti's.

ARCADIPANE: Oh yes, his mother. Yes, I know. Seems she's in a bad way.

GIONNI: Yes, I'm afraid so. I just stopped off in passing to let you know that . . .

ARCADIPANE: Wait a minute. I'll call Sara. [*He goes over to the door Left, mounts the step, and calls*] Come down a minute,

Sara . . . The doctor's here. [SARA *comes in through the door Left.*]

SARA [*apprehensively*]: What's happened now?

GIONNI: Nothing. Now don't get agitated. I only want to tell Lucio something . . . So that he's prepared . . .

SARA: He must be upstairs, Lucio. Strange he didn't hear the carriage-bells.

GIONNI: He's probably asleep.

SARA: No. Would to God he were! He doesn't sleep a wink. Oh, believe me, I'm so very worried about him. And now, on top of it all, this accident to his father . . .

GIONNI: Yes, but that's all . . .

SARA: You can have no idea how his poor head . . .

ARCADIPANE: He never gives himself a moment's rest . . .

SARA: Oh, and his eyes . . . I don't know how to put it . . . It's as if they were petrified . . . Yes, that's it! . . . Petrified with grief! . . . And yet . . . They're *blazing* at the same time . . . As though he were in a raging fever. And what he must be thinking! Last night he told me that it might well be that the hour of his father's resurrection was at hand.

ARCADIPANE: What did he mean by that? Hasn't he risen already? By means of the miracle . . . [*A gesture in the direction of* GIONNI].

GIONNI: For pity's sake, don't call it a miracle! Don't *you* call it a miracle too!

ARCADIPANE: But that's what everybody's calling it! Everybody!

GIONNI: And that's what's so harmful! We must put a stop to it!

ARCADIPANE: Harmful, do you call it? Why, we're all still absolutely flabbergasted by it! There's talk of nothing else in the whole countryside hereabouts.

SARA: And you can just imagine what it's like in town!

GIONNI: Oh yes, I dare say! But now just think of what it

means for him. I mean, what we have to fear as the possible consequences for him . . . Precisely because there *is* all this to-do.

ARCADIPANE: You mean because everybody's going around shouting about the miracle of his resurrection?

GIONNI: Exactly. Precisely. He cannot possibly admit that it's true . . . Believing as he believes, he just cannot admit the possibility of such a miracle as this.

ARCADIPANE: And why can't he?

GIONNI: Because God alone can call the dead back to life.

ARCADIPANE: I still can't see why he can't believe in it. Wasn't this, maybe, the Will of God?

GIONNI: Ah, there you have it! Good for you, Arcadipane! So I'm not a devil in *your* eyes?

ARCADIPANE: What on earth are you saying, Doctor?

GIONNI: I see everybody eyeing me, just as if I possessed the diabolical power of bringing the dead back to life . . .

ARCADIPANE: Well, you know, you have brought *one* back!

GIONNI: Precisely! By means of a miracle! And it's this very man, who ought to be thanking God that I did, who's keeping me on tenterhooks, in case he should get to know what's happened!

SARA: Oh, then perhaps that's why Lucio says . . .

GIONNI: What?

SARA: That his father's true resurrection is at hand?

GIONNI: Does he suppose that his father will himself admit it in the end?

SARA: Perhaps he *hopes* he will.

GIONNI: He'd do well not to build his hopes too high. As a matter of fact I came here on purpose to warn him as to what attitude to adopt with his father, when he comes. And I'd like to warn you too . . .

SARA: Oh, there's no need to warn us. We shan't be seeing him, Doctor. We shall be gone before he gets here . . .

ARCADIPANE: We're just on the point of going now . . .

GIONNI: Oh, of course, yes. Forgive me . . .

SARA: I'll go up. I'll just go up and call Lucio. [*She crosses the stage and exit, going up the stairs Right.*]

GIONNI: Ah, yes! I know! I've done you a bad turn, Arcadipane. Naturally, when the news of his death reached you . . .

ARCADIPANE: You mustn't think, Doctor, that Sara and I rejoiced at it . . .

GIONNI: I don't say you *rejoiced* . . . But it's quite certain it left you in a position to . . .

ARCADIPANE: To regularize our union? Ah, yes! We'd have done that at once . . .

GIONNI [*almost to himself*]: That's curious!

ARCADIPANE: What is?

GIONNI: You still could . . .

ARCADIPANE: *How* could we? With him alive?

GIONNI: There's the death-certificate.

ARCADIPANE: It'll be cancelled!

GIONNI: But at the moment it's still valid . . . All signed, sealed and delivered by the doctor who made the post-mortem examination. *Legally* he's dead.

ARCADIPANE: You don't mean that seriously . . .

GIONNI: No . . . But he's certainly . . . In the eyes of the law . . .

ARCADIPANE: The law, Doctor . . . There's only one law . . . The Law of God.

GIONNI: But your children . . .

ARCADIPANE: It'll be sufficient for them not to be outside God's Law. I've got nothing to leave them, except the example of obedience to that Law. There's only one thing that grieves my heart . . . That I shall never again hear my own voice under the tiles of this roof. It brings back to me . . . Oh, if you only knew! . . . The memory of so many nights. Sitting on that step over there. Gazing over at the staircase. Oh, you can't possibly imagine the love that I've been able *to put into* these stones . . . Into this earth . . . Into every tree that I've planted here . . . With her by my side . . . [*He is alluding to* SARA.] She stepped down from being my Master's wife and became my comrade. Here she comes now . . . She's coming downstairs with her son. I'll be going. I've never spoken to him in my life. I've never even let him catch sight of me.

[*He goes out Back, turning to the Left.* LUCIO *and* SARA *come down the stairs Right.* LUCIO *is twenty-two, slim and very pale, with a face hollowed by the spiritual travail that has kindled a feverish light in his eyes. He has slender, graceful, and very sensitive hands. At frequent intervals he wrings them convulsively. He is not at all shy. On the contrary, it's as if he were impelled to speech and action by an anxiety which seems at times to be instinct with anger. He's rather ill at ease in the clothes he's wearing – a grey, ready-made suit, somewhat clumsy in cut. He looks rather like a schoolboy who's wearing long trousers for the first time. He comes hurrying down the stairs with his mother.*]

LUCIO: No, no, Doctor . . . !

GIONNI: Good morning, Lucio . . .

LUCIO: Good morning. I cannot remain silent! I give you fair warning . . . I cannot remain silent! If he comes here . . .

GIONNI: All that I meant was . . . With regard to what's happened.

LUCIO: What is it that you want me not to tell him?

GIONNI: Why . . . This thing that everybody's calling a miracle . . . The help I gave . . .

LUCIO: And why shouldn't I mention it to him?

GIONNI: Because he doesn't know anything about it yet!

LUCIO: He doesn't know anything about it . . . ?

SARA: He doesn't know that it was you who . . . ?

GIONNI: For pity's sake, not a word about *that*! He remembers nothing whatsoever about anything. All he knows is that he was knocked down by a motor-car. He thinks that he was concussed and that his memory of everything has been completely blotted out.

SARA: He doesn't even know about the death-certificate, then?

GIONNI: He knows nothing about anything! Nothing at all! I tell you, he hasn't even the remotest suspicion. He's busy thanking God that, apart from the concussion ... Oh yes, that might very well have proved fatal! ... He suffered no other harm as a result of being knocked down.

LUCIO: And do you really think it's possible that he won't find out what's happened?

GIONNI: The most important thing is that he shan't find out about it for the moment ... Not in the state that he's in just now. You can imagine the effect it would have on his mind, can't you? ... His spiritual agony ...

LUCIO: You don't think it would do him good to know?

GIONNI: Good heavens, no! God forbid! You'd better get that idea out of your head as quickly as possible! He damned me as a sacrilegious scoundrel merely for bringing a dead *rabbit* back to life! Just imagine what he'd have to say now, if he found out that ... ! I give you my solemn oath, Lucio, that if it hadn't been for your little sister ... Who implored me to do the same thing for him ... She was absolutely desperate! ... Well, as far as my own predilections are concerned, I'd have thought twice about it ... And more than twice ... Before doing it. Yes, I'd have had serious scruples about doing it ... Just *because* of what the consequences were likely to be ...

LUCIO: And suppose it's ... *Those consequences* ... That I'm relying on now?

GIONNI: No! No! What on earth are you talking about? You're *relying* on the consequences ... ?

LUCIO: I'm relying on those consequences to call him back to life, and to ensure that God shall really and truly accom-

plish His miracle ... In this body of my father's, which has
once more been made to arise and walk.

GIONNI: You're willing, then, to run the risk of killing him?

LUCIO: 'Am I ...'? No, Doctor. *You're* the one that's running
that risk, not *me*.

GIONNI: How am I? Why do you say that?

LUCIO: You have set upon his feet ... And made to walk
again ... *What?* ... Merely a body?

GIONNI: A *body*? But your father has his faith!

LUCIO: Precisely. And did you show any respect for that
faith of his when you set him on his feet again, using means
which he regards as sacrilegious? The moment he finds out
the truth, *you* will have killed him!

GIONNI: But surely ... Well, this is certainly how it seems
to me! ... Surely at this very moment I'm doing all I
possibly can to *prevent* ...

LUCIO: To prevent his finding out? If he doesn't find out
today he'll do so tomorrow.

GIONNI: All I'm asking is that he shouldn't find out at this
precise moment. Do remember that, after all, it was on
your account ...

LUCIO: You mustn't say that it was on my account! You
mustn't say that it was on my account! Say rather that it
was so that this supreme test ... The supreme test of life
itself ... Which God has been pleased to visit both upon
him and upon me ... Might be met.

GIONNI [*shrugging his shoulders*]: Supreme test ... Supreme
test ...

LUCIO: Do you mean you think it's something more important than that? Doctor, you mustn't do anything to hinder
him in any way, if he should come up here today in order
to face it.

GIONNI: But do you really imagine that that's what he's
coming for?

LUCIO: *Isn't* he coming up here in order to speak with me?

GIONNI: Yes, but I'm quite sure that he's not expecting to have to face this supreme test that you've been talking about! Not in the least!

LUCIO: What is he expecting then?

GIONNI: *I don't know!* I suppose that ... Well, that he's expecting you to retract ...

LUCIO: To go back on what I've done? And do you mean to say that you expect me not to tell him what my reasons were for doing what I have done?

GIONNI [*getting angry*]: Oh, go on! Tell him your reasons! Do whatever you think best! It'll all seem like heresy to him, anyway! You know, when all's said and done, my dear Lucio, mine's a rum fate, and no mistake! Look at me! *Doomed!* Doomed to get everybody's back up! All the time! It must be my face ... I don't know ... Perhaps it's my voice. I respect other people's faith, and at the same time people get annoyed with me on account of my tolerance! I think like you, I feel like you. And here we both are: you're thoroughly annoyed with me, and I'm thoroughly annoyed with you ... !

LUCIO [*smiling*]: No. You're wrong there, I'm not the least bit annoyed ...

GIONNI: *I* am, though! And I'm going! I've done my duty as a doctor. I implore you ... As a friend ... To leave your father in ignorance. Just for the moment. Leave him in ignorance of what's happened to him.

SARA: Yes! Yes! I agree with what you say! You oughtn't to tell him anything. Not just for the present.

LUCIO: If you think that it'll do him the slightest harm, I'll keep silent, even if he forces me to talk about ...

GIONNI: That's not what I'm saying!

LUCIO: I shall have to, Doctor! He'll want to talk to me about my loss of faith, and I shall then be obliged to answer that it's not true that I've lost my faith. And that, as a matter of fact, I've acquired it, if anything ...

GIONNI: Not as far as he's concerned. No, you haven't acquired it . . .

LUCIO: Faith is something that everyone acquires for himself . . .

GIONNI: No . . . I mean . . . Well, the way he looks at things . . .

LUCIO: And do you know how I've acquired it? Simply by denying the reality of that death you're so frightened he'll get to hear about . . .

GIONNI: *Denying* it? How can you deny *death*?

LUCIO: By ceasing to presume that God, simply because this body of mine will tomorrow . . . In the natural course of events . . . Fall to the ground, like a withered leaf from off the bough . . .

GIONNI: And isn't that death?

LUCIO: Why, of course it isn't! What do you mean, Doctor . . . *Death!* A handful of dust that returns to dust . . .

GIONNI: That's what your father says, too!

LUCIO: Yes . . . But he goes on to assume that . . .

GIONNI: Yes, quite! That his spirit . . .

LUCIO: *His* spirit? How is it *his*? You see . . . Don't you? That's where he's in error!

SARA: In saying that it's *his* spirit?

LUCIO: Yes, that's it, Mummy! In admitting that it is eternal . . . Infinite . . . And yet assuming that it can possibly be *mine* . . . Something that belongs to a man who dwells within the boundaries of time . . . A fleeting, momentary form . . . Something that is yesterday's or tomorrow's. You see how it is, don't you? So that we may not ourselves come to an end, we annihilate life. In God's name. And we make God to rule over the kingdom that lies beyond this world. No one knows where it is. We make Him rule there too. Over a kingdom of the dead which we have imagined in order that, when we reach it, He may give us our reward or our punishment. Almost as if Good and Evil could, by

185

some strange possibility, be good and evil as they are known by a creature who is but a *part* . . . Whilst He alone, Who is the Whole . . . He alone knows what it is that He does and why He does it. There, do you see, Doctor? This thing ought to be for him, as it has been for me, a true resurrection from the dead. He must deny that there is death in God. He must believe in this, which is the only Immortality that there is. An Immortality that is not our own, not something that is in or for ourselves. That is not the hope of reward or the fear of punishment. He must believe in the eternal present of life . . . Which is God . . . And that shall suffice. And then indeed will God . . . After this experience which He has vouchsafed that my father shall undergo . . . Then will He . . . And He alone . . . Accomplish the miracle of his resurrection. I shall say nothing, nothing at all. Nothing, I promise you. I shall let him say just whatever he wishes to say to me. And . . . Don't worry, I'll do everything within my power to avoid sharing your fate, Doctor. I mean, I'll try to say nothing that might irritate him.

GIONNI [*he is lost in wonder and admiration at what* LUCIO *has so gently, so fervently and so simply said*]: Exactly! Provided, of course, that by keeping quiet you don't irritate him all the more. That's what you might call *my* fate! Take *now*, for instance . . . I'm irritated to the point of exasperation with myself for the advice I've been giving you. Oh well, don't let's say any more on that subject. Let's hope that everything turns out well in the end. Good-bye for the moment, Mrs . . .

SARA: Good-bye. But you must call me Sara . . . Don't call me Mrs anything at all. Will you be coming back?

GIONNI: Oh, yes! Yes! Very soon. Good-bye then. [*Exit Back, taking the left turn. Shortly after he disappears you hear the sound of his carriage-bells.*]

SARA: And now I'll be going as well . . .

LUCIO [*hearing the sound*]: Can you hear, Mummy?

SARA: Hear what?

LUCIO: Those bells.

SARA: It'll be the Doctor's carriage.

LUCIO: When I was a little boy I used to think that the open country, stretched out there in the morning sunlight, was made especially to spread the sound of the festive bells.

SARA: The country? But, my dear, when you were a little boy . . .

LUCIO: I could see it from the courtyard of the seminary, way up there at San Gerlando. I used to look down on to it. The other boys . . . At playtime . . . Used to race about . . . Shouting like mad, and tucking up their cassocks so as to be able to run better. I used to keep in the background. At the end of the yard. Because from there I could enjoy the wide sweeping vista of the green valley. With the great wide road that cut through it like a furrow. And I could see the carriages driving out through the countryside . . . Ever so tiny they looked . . . Three horses harnessed to-gether . . . And from far far away there would come stealing up on me . . . Yes, just as it's doing at this very moment . . . That sound of bells. [*His mother is in tears; he turns to her*] Are you crying, Mummy?

SARA: Yes, because of the grief that I can hear in your voice . . .

LUCIO: Yes, I did feel . . . I did feel a terrible anguish . . . Anguish . . . Regret for life, which might have been so lovely. It seemed to me that I was experiencing all the joyfulness of a drive in the open air . . . Through the countryside . . . Through those green fields . . . All golden in the sunlight. I feel so strongly the sensations that belong to places . . . And the smells of things. I think of how we used to come out of the seminary, two by two, as we went out for our walks. And we'd pass by one of those carriages standing on the rank in the Square . . . Waiting to be hired. You know, I can still smell the reek of stables. I can even see a wisp of straw between the horses' grey lips. I can hear the ring of their iron-shod hooves on the cobbles when they stamped. You see, Mummy, when I was a little boy, up there in the seminary, faith was ... It was *smell* ... Taste ... The smell of incense ... The smell of wax ... The taste of the Consecrated Host ... And a terrible dismay at people's footsteps as they echoed inside the empty church ...

SARA: You were very tiny ... Your little face was so very white even then ... Oh, how it hurt me, my son, when I saw you come home for the holidays, dressed in your little cassock! *You* used to tuck your cassock up too ... So that you could run to me ... And then you'd immediately let it drop again ... So that the little girls in the street shouldn't laugh at you ... And shout after you, 'Little priesty! Little priesty!' And it was as if your eyes were filled with terror when you looked at me ...

LUCIO [*covering his eyes with his hands*]: No, Mummy! *No!* Don't remind me!

SARA: Why not?

LUCIO: If you only knew the shame of it all! Why there *was* that look in my eyes. All the filth of life! Child as I was, I had absorbed into myself all the filth of life! It had been put there inside me by one of the boys ... One of the big boys. You know the one I mean, don't you? He went mad later on. His name was Spano ... That was the one.

SARA: You were barely six years old ...

LUCIO: And I knew everything! And I don't know whether it was more horror I felt, or *terror*. Terror of that evil beast who defiled everything with his foul imagination, and who spared nobody!

SARA: Did he talk to you about me? Oh, the vile creature!

LUCIO: You can have no conception of the way he terrorized me! He did just whatever he liked with me! He simply terrified me!

SARA: Oh, I never suspected *that*! I never dreamt that things were as bad as that!

LUCIO: If you'd only known...

SARA: I saw that you were crushed... Mortified... As a child of your age ought never to be. But I should never, never, have guessed that that was why! It used to tear my heart to shreds within me to see you two children, you and her, the way you were... Dear, tender creatures... Wilting away. And it grieved my heart to see your father so hard, so obstinate, so determined not to admit that I was right. Though it just wasn't possible... I'm sure of that now... That he wasn't suffering too. He would tell me that you were both well...

LUCIO: Indeed? *Well!*

SARA: Yes, well. And I... I would take your little faces in my hands and make him look at them. 'Do you still dare to tell me that they're well?' I felt that the life I was leading ... Well, I couldn't stand it any longer. I felt the tortures that were being inflicted upon you... I felt them as if they were biting into my own flesh.

LUCIO: Yes. And when, in point of fact, poor Lia...

SARA: When I saw them bring her back home to me... A helpless cripple... Her life – *finished*... And when I saw that the Sisters... The very Sisters who were to blame for my child's being in that terrible condition... Were to help me look after her...

LUCIO: They were...?

SARA: Yes, you understand... *They* were to... I wasn't to be left to look after her myself! They were the ones who were to...! I hurled myself at one of them, just like a wild beast... Oh, I don't know what I did to her! They tore her from my grasp... They thought I was possessed by a devil [*She breaks off, so that she may curb the frantic onrush of hatred which she feels once more assailing her. She begins again immediately*] Lucio, they made me go away... They forced me to run away... Just as if I'd been a madwoman! I begged them, I implored them to bring my baby up here to me . . . I was quite sure that I'd have been able to make her well again. But I had to have her up here by herself . . . Without him. I couldn't bear the sight of him any longer . . . I'd have killed him! He wanted me back again. Yes, because . . . He posed as a saint . . . Set himself up as a tyrant . . . And then . . . Well, what made me most furious with him . . . Whenever he came near me . . . Was the feebleness, the softness of the man . . . [*She breaks off with an exclamation and gesture of disgust*] Oh, God! . . . And yet, I swear to you, Lucio, I'd have made the sacrifice . . . I'd have made the sacrifice . . . I'd have overcome the horror that I felt for him from that time on . . . Provided that some good might have come out of it . . . For *you* . . . For you, my children. And I stipulated that you at least should be set free and allowed to come and live up here . . . You and Lia . . . Up here with me. He refused . . . He wouldn't hear of it. And so . . . He refused what I demanded, and I refused his demands! You cannot imagine what I suffered! My agony here . . . And yours there in the seminary! And even if I'd sacrificed myself I couldn't have brought you one moment's solace in that agony of yours.

LUCIO: I know that you applied to the Courts . . .

SARA: And they decided against me.

LUCIO: They decided against you?

SARA: Yes, they decided against me! They said that it was my duty to remain with him and my daughter! And that my claim that you ought to be taken away from the seminary was an unjust one. And, to cut a long story short, that it was *I* . . . I, and not he . . . Who was breaking up the family. I was so furious . . . After two years of desperate, ferocious struggle . . . That I threw up everything . . . Everything! What else was I to do? I felt such a loathing! You can see the town from up here. I couldn't bear the sight of it any longer. I turned my face away whenever my eyes . . . Against my will . . . Strayed in that direction! I

felt such a loathing for those churches ... Those houses ...
And the Court that ... All of them! When they deny a
mother the right to look after her own children ... When
a mother who is trying to provide for the health of her
own children is condemned in Court ... You can't help
yourself. Life becomes impossible. They condemn you to
act as I acted! I threw away everything I possessed and
became a peasant. A peasant! Up here ... Out in the open
air ... Out in the scorching sun! ... I was seized with the
need ... The overwhelming *need* ... To be a savage! ...
I felt the need to sink down to the ground at nightfall ...
Like a beast that's been worked to death. Hoeing, treading
out the grain on the threshing-floor with the mules ...
Barefoot in the August sun ... Tramping round and round,
with my legs bleeding ... And shouting like a drunkard!
I felt the need to be brutal with everyone who asked me to
have compassion on myself ... You know who I mean!
This pure man. He's as pure, Lucio, as a babe newly
delivered from the Hands of God. This man ... Who's
never been able to endure my setting myself on the same
level as himself ... And who prevented me from destroying
myself ... By teaching me all the secrets of the countryside ... All the secrets of life ... The *true* life that's lived
out here ... Far far away from the cursèd town ... The
true life that is the life of the earth. This life which now I
feel ... Because my hands tend it ... Help it to grow, to
flower and to bear fruit. And the joy of the rain that comes
just at the right moment. And the calamity of the mist that
makes the olives wilt, just as they are about to burst into
flower ... And ... Have you seen the grass that grows on
the bank at the side of the lane here? So fresh and green at
daybreak, when the rime's upon it! And the pleasure ...
You know, it's something so wonderful! ... The sheer
pleasure of making bread with the same hands that sowed
the corn ... !

LUCIO: Yes, Mummy! *Yes!* And, as you see, I've come to you...

SARA: My son, the joy you've given me, God alone ... God Who sent you to me ... He alone could bestow it on me. And I shouted, I shouted in your father's face that I felt myself once again to be blessèd among women ... *Purified!* You've paid me back in full, my son ... For everything ... With your coming. And, as you see, I too can speak to you about everything. Without being puffed up with pride or cast down with shame. Because I alone know what I've had to suffer ... What price it is that I've had to pay ... In order that I might become what I now am ... Something that perhaps nobody any longer knows the meaning of ... Something ... *Natural.*

LUCIO: *I* do. I understand the meaning of what you are. When I see you before me ... When I hear you speak ...

SARA: I really *have* set myself free. There's nothing I desire, because there's nothing I lack. I hope for nothing, because what I have is sufficient for my needs. My health is sound, my heart's at peace with the world, and my mind is serene.

LUCIO: But, Mummy, you can't, you *mustn't* go away from here.

SARA: I've already gone. All my things are on their way to...

LUCIO: No, no! I'll stop it! Yes, this is something that I *shall* talk to him about! And I shan't mince my words!

SARA: You can't do anything to stop it, Lucio ...

LUCIO: Yes, I can, I tell you! I *must!*

SARA: You cannot and you must not! No! And, what's more, I don't want you to. *I don't want you to.*

LUCIO: But all that you've done up here ...

SARA: It wasn't for my own sake that I did it. I should like ... Yes, it's true – and I said as much to your father ... I should like to think that what I'd done, I'd done for your sake, yours and Lia's. Yes, that is something you *can* try to stop him from doing. I mean, stop him from letting the farm ... All the wealth of this farm ... Go to rack and ruin. As it most certainly will if there's nobody here who's really competent to look after it. You still have the right to forbid him to do that with the property. If you can't do it on your own behalf, you can at least do it on behalf of your little sister. But you can't do it for my sake . . . And you *mustn't*. I repeat . . . *I don't want you to.*

LUCIO: It shall be as you wish. I'll do it for my own and Lia's sake. But you . . . Where will you go?

SARA: Don't worry about me. We've made all our arrangements. We know where we're going. Just for the present we're going to stay with one of our friends who's bailiff on a farm some little way from here – at Le Favare. Then next year we're going to be leased a farm . . . It's quite near here. And then there'll be a chance of making a little for ourselves . . . Because up to now, you know, we've never kept a pennypiece for ourselves. But we shall have to start putting something aside . . .

LUCIO: Yes, you will, because . . . Mummy, do forgive me . . . I've not yet had the courage to talk to you about it . . . You've got two children . . .

SARA: Yes, *his* children. You haven't seen them yet, of course. They're two sturdy little peasants . . . Baked brown by the sun.

LUCIO: And he . . .

SARA: Oh, if you only knew how apprehensive you make him . . . How you terrify him . . .

LUCIO: *I* do . . . ?

SARA: Yes . . . He's afraid, and he's ashamed. He's counting the seconds. He's simply dying to get clear of this place. He knows that I'm talking to you at this moment, and I'm quite sure that he's out there, and behaving just like a bitch with a litter of puppies! You know, her master's picked one of them up to show a friend, and she doesn't dare snarl at him! She just keeps on stealing pitiful glances at them, to see what they're doing to her baby . . .

LUCIO: Won't you call him in?

SARA: Why? Would you like me to?

LUCIO: Yes. And the children too.

SARA: They're probably just outside . . . They're waiting for me, so that they can make a start. [*She goes to the back of the stage and calls out towards the Right*] Oh, Roro! Come on in, will you? Yes, in here! Come on! And bring the children! Come on! Come on!

LUCIO: You call him Roro?

SARA: Yes, that's *my* name for him. His real name's Rosario, and I call him Roro. The little one was already up on the mule. As soon as he finds himself in the saddle, that lad's as happy as a sandboy!

LUCIO: What are the children's names?

SARA: Tonotto . . . That's the elder one . . . And the other one's Michele. Here they come now. [ARCADIPANE *enters back, leading the two little boys by the hand.*] This is Arcadipane. [*The two boys run to her.* TONOTTO *reaches her first, then* MICHELE.] And this is Tonotto. And this [*she takes the younger boy in her arms*] . . . Is Michele.

LUCIO: [*bending down to kiss* TONOTTO, *and then kissing* MICHELE *as he perches there in his mother's arms*]: How lovely they are, Mummy! So strong!

SARA: They're healthy. [*To* ARCADIPANE] You don't remember Lucio, do you?

ARCADIPANE: Oh, yes. I remember him as a little chap . . . No bigger than him. [*Pointing to* TONOTTO.]

LUCIO: I've got a memory of those days too . . . But I don't know whether it's really true or not . . . It's a memory of you too, Mummy. But perhaps it's not really a memory . . . Perhaps it's a vision that came to me . . . I don't know . . . As though from another life . . . Like when in a dream you're looking out of a window that's ever so far away . . . And sunk deep in the world of your dream. But seeing you again now . . . I don't know . . . I find myself beginning to doubt whether . . .

SARA: But of course I'm quite a different woman now, as you know very well!

LUCIO: Oh, yes! Of course! But, as I was saying . . . What I'm beginning to doubt . . . Well, I'm beginning to wonder whether that picture of you was not just something that I'd dreamt. It showed you as so very different . . . Someone quite else . . . No, not more beautiful, Mummy, you know . . . Quite the contrary, in point of fact! You're so lovely now . . . So very much, so very very much more lovely! And the woman of my vision . . . She, on the other hand, was so very sad. And the picture of him, too, the one that I carried in my mind . . . But tell me something, Mummy . . . Don't laugh! . . . Don't you remember . . . When we were at home . . . When you were still living with us . . . We had a cat . . . She was all white . . . ?

SARA: A white cat? When you . . . ? [*Suddenly she remembers: she sees the picture* . . .] Yes! Yes! We did! We did have a . . . ! But it wasn't a *she*, it was a *tom*! Yes, we did have one . . . Yes! Yes! It was white . . . A lovely big white tomcat. Why, yes! Yes, I remember!

LUCIO: In that case . . .

SARA: In that case *what*?

LUCIO: The thing I've been remembering all this time must be a picture of you. Yes. A room . . . A dining-room . . . Very large . . . With a low ceiling . . .

SARA: Why, yes! The dining-room in the house we used to live in . . .

ARCADIPANE: At the bottom of the path leading up to San Francesco . . .

LUCIO: I don't remember it at all clearly . . . I've only got . . . Well, a vague impression of that room . . .

SARA: Yes, it had a window looking out on to the vegetable gardens over the road . . .

LUCIO: There was a square table in the middle of the room . . . I can see it now . . . With just one place laid . . . A table-napkin . . . Freshly-ironed and with the folds still showing stiffly . . . A bottle of red wine, with the froth in the neck of the bottle . . . I could catch it on my fingers . . . Just like this! . . . That sunbeam which was playing down upon it, through a chink in the closed shutters across the window! . . . He's sitting there . . . Where that table-napkin is . . . And eating, with his head bowed over his plate . . . The white cat is sitting there too, perched up on the other side of the table . . . His front legs are stiff, his head high . . . His tail is hanging down over the edge of the table, and every now and again it moves . . . Just as if it were moving of its own accord . . . Like a little snake. And, Mummy, you're talking to *him*, and not paying any attention to me . . . Suddenly you turn round, fall down on your knees and take me in your arms . . . And . . . I don't know why . . . You burst into tears . . . Holding me ever so tightly to your breast. I stick my head over your shoulder . . . So as to look at him . . . Just as if the suspicion's dawned on me that it was he who'd made you cry. I see him get up from the table . . . Abruptly . . . And his eyes too are red with tears . . . He goes over to the corner of the room . . . Picks up a gun that's leaning against the wall . . . And dashes out of the room. I'm terribly afraid, and I'm just going to scream out when, Mummy, you suddenly let go of me and rush out of the room after him. I'm left there . . . In a state of suspense and bewildered dismay. And then I see the cat jump across to where the plate is . . . Snatch up the meat in its teeth . . . And jump down from the table. It's curious how vivid my memory still is of that cat . . . Whilst the pictures I have of you . . . Of him and of you . . . I can remember very clearly how you were both crying.

SARA: It was on your account, my son. I was crying because of you . . . And so was he.

ARCADIPANE: She was crying because of what she was suffering . . .

SARA: I was in such a state that I just had to pour out my heart to anyone that came along . . .

ARCADIPANE: Everybody was sorry for her!

SARA: Lucio, there's something I'm going to tell you now . . . Here in front of him. I've never said it to anyone before . . . Not even to myself. When, in utter desperation, I left the house and came up here . . . I knew quite well . . . I'd become aware that, under the compassion that he felt for me, there lay . . . Already . . . A feeling of affection for me . . . [*Turning* towards ARCADIPANE] Tell me . . . Wasn't there? It's true, isn't it?

ARCADIPANE [*his bashfulness assails him again; he gives assent more by his nod than by his barely audible*]: Yes, its true . . .

SARA: A woman is very quick to notice such things, even if she pretends not to have noticed them, and goes on treating the man as I managed then to go on treating *him* . . .

ARCADIPANE: I was her servant . . . And I swear that even what I felt then . . .

SARA: There's no need for you to swear anything of the kind. As you'll remember, I began by telling you that what I'm saying now is something that I'm revealing for the first time to myself . . . And you didn't want to either . . . Did you? . . . You didn't want to admit to yourself that you were in love with me?

ARCADIPANE: I was afraid to . . . !

SARA: Very well then. And now I must confess that it was this very thing, this secret awareness of his love, Lucio, that drew me to the land . . . That made me want to live the life of a peasant. And I was like him – I didn't want to admit it to myself either. Rather as if it were some kind of folly that I was bent on committing. But feeling deep down inside me that this was the only way in which I could keep myself from going mad . . . Yes, the only way! . . . By acting furiously the part of a peasant-woman! And that's why I was always so rude to *him* . . . When he still wouldn't understand . . . Still tried to prevent me from doing what I wanted to do! And now it's your turn, Lucio, to realize that . . . Having made a clean break in my life . . . As I was forced to do . . . I can't find any place for you in my present life. You come back to me out of that life, the life that is no longer *my* life, my son, and I can't find any room for you in my present life. It belongs to him and to these two little children. I must, I *must* go with them.

LUCIO: Yes, Mummy, that's only what's right. And you mustn't think that I want . . . Or hoped that my coming here . . .

SARA: I know, Lucio. I'm only saying all this so as to give him the strength to face up to you. [*To* ARCADIPANE] And now we must be going.

LUCIO: I know too that I may not even so much as come with you . . .

SARA: No, Lucio, you can't . . .

LUCIO: But I should like you at least to . . .

SARA: To what? Tell me . . . Tell me . . .

LUCIO: Well . . . I mean . . . Secretly, if you like, Mummy . . .

SARA: Secretly? . . . I? . . .

LUCIO: Yes. I want you to give me the strength . . . After I've had my talk with him . . . To set out on my new path . . . Alone . . . As I must be . . . And without any longer having anybody to help me . . . Without even a proper place in society.

SARA: But why . . . ? Of course you won't be . . . Why should you? Don't you want to stay . . . ?

LUCIO: Stay where? In the same house as my father? Like this? [*He points to his lay attire.*] You know what he's like!

SARA: But he can't turn you out!

LUCIO: No, he can't turn me out. But he certainly won't want any longer to give me the money to go and finish my studies . . .

SARA: I'll give you the money if he refuses! No matter what it costs me!

LUCIO: No, Mummy, you can't . . .

SARA: I can . . . Oh yes, I can! No matter what it costs me, I tell you!

LUCIO: No, you can't. What I mean is . . . You *can't* . . . For the same reason that I can't come away with you, Mummy.

SARA: But it's not the same thing at all! No! If you were to take the money from him . . . [*A gesture in the direction of* ARCADIPANE.] But you'll get it from me, from what I earn with my work.

LUCIO: You owe everything that you earn by your work to your children. No. And, what's more, perhaps it's all for the best that I should give up studying and make some attempt to free myself . . . Just as you have done . . .

SARA: No! No!

LUCIO: Yes! So that I too may find my own true nature . . .

SARA: No!

LUCIO: So that my life too may become simple and easy in the humility of toiling with my hands . . .

SARA: But you won't be able to . . . !

LUCIO: Oh yes, I shall! I shall . . . !

SARA: You won't be strong enough to . . .

LUCIO: I shall find strength . . .

SARA: No . . . No . . . You must do good in life in another way . . . Oh, my son! . . . Using the light that shines here . . . Here behind your brow . . .

LUCIO: I shall still be able to do good in that way, even when I'm toiling away as a humble labourer.

SARA: No, you mustn't. In this matter you're not to take me as your example. No. I was able to do what I've done because only by so doing could I find my deliverance and my salvation. But you're different . . . There are so many paths before you.

LUCIO: At the moment I can't see one single one.

SARA: If you've found yourself unable to follow the path on

which he chose to set you when you were a child, it'll be his bounden *duty* . . . Now . . . To give you both the time and the means to find some other path . . . One that is worthy of you . . . One along which you may walk . . . One that will carry you far!

LUCIO: Yes, you're quite right, Mummy. But I didn't mean just talking about me . . . I meant, talking about . . . *Everything*. I stand in need of comfort at this moment, and you alone can bring me the comfort I need. I've come to you, defying everybody and everything, simply in order to obtain that comfort.

SARA: Yes . . . Yes . . . Tell me . . . What is this comfort?

LUCIO: I want to feel that you're near me – even if you're hidden – when I have my talk with him. Perhaps it's so that I shan't say things which I ought not to say. I need this strength to come to me from you. Don't deny me it. Then you shall go away. No one shall prevent you. No one shall see you go.

SARA: Very well, Lucio, if that's what you want me to . . .

ARCADIPANE [*apprehensively*]: But hidden . . . *Where?*

SARA: No . . . Not hidden. Why should I hide? I've seen him already, and talked to him face to face. And, if the need were to arise, I shouldn't find myself at a loss in having to talk to him again. I'll wait up there . . . The rooms are all empty. He'll never dream that I'd want to stay here. There's not even a chair left up there. I'll sit on the little ledge under the window, and wait till you've finished your talk.

ARCADIPANE: No, Sara . . . Don't do it!

SARA: What are you afraid of?

LUCIO: I'll answer for her. She'll come away with me. She shall return to her sons and to you. You need have no worries on that score.

ARCADIPANE [*to* SARA]: But won't *he* think that Lucio's defending the land for your sake too, if you stay here?

SARA: I've already told him to his face that we don't need his farm to keep us alive ... Seeing that we've never taken anything out of it ...

LUCIO: And I shall do nothing to prevent him from disposing of it just as he wishes. Don't worry. I repeat, I can't go on living in the same house with him. I shall go away too. Besides, Mummy, it doesn't matter really ... You go ... You go on your way ... With him . ... I'll find my own strength.

SARA: No! No! I'll stay! I'll stay ... I'll go upstairs. [*The sound of carriage-bells is heard.*] You go on ... Go on. Wait for me at Lotti's Farm ... I'll rejoin you there. If it's not Dr Gionni on his way back, it'll be them. Go on! ... Go on! [ARCADIPANE *and the two little boys exeunt back. The noise of the bells comes nearer.* SARA *goes over to the door Left, and before she goes off she says to* LUCIO] I am here, my son. [*Exit, closing the door behind her.*]

[LUCIO *stands there expectantly. Shortly afterwards the carriage stops outside the house.* CICO'S *voice is heard.*]

CICO: Here we are! Here we are! Your carriage awaits! I'll help you down! I'll help you down!

DEODATA: No! Take it easy! No! Let me do it, Cico! I know how to lift her.

CICO: Your carriage is all ready! There's a good girl! There she goes ... Racing along as if it was her own two little legs that were carrying her!

[LIA *comes into sight in her wheel-chair. She is silhouetted against the sunlight at the back of the stage.* CICO *and* DEODATA *come running in after her.*]

LIA: Lucio! Lucio! Where are you?

LUCIO [*running over and embracing her*]: Here I am, Lia!

DEODATA [*her first astonishment is rapidly extinguished by a sense of disillusionment, which is near to contempt*]: There he is!

CICO: Oh, look! I didn't even notice ...

LIA [*freeing herself from his embrace*]: Let me look at you!

No-o-o-o. You look silly! Oh, dear, you look as if you've shrunk!

DEODATA: You've got the nerve to show yourself in those clothes . . . ?

CICO: He might be just anybody . . .

LIA: You don't look like *you* any longer!

DEODATA: If you only knew the effect you have on people who see you again looking like this, after . . . ! But where on earth did you buy that suit? Can't you see how badly it's gaping open round the neck?

LUCIO: What does that matter? Where's my father? Isn't he coming?

LIA: Yes, he's coming . . . With Monsignor Lelli . . . In another carriage. They were waiting for the lawyer.

LUCIO: So that they could settle the transfer of the farm?

DEODATA: Oh, just think of it! The moment he claps eyes on you, looking like that! He won't want to listen to a word you've got to say. And meanwhile, just you take a look at her . . . [*She takes* LIA's *face between her hands, and shows it to* LUCIO.] It's done her good already . . . The first breath of fresh air, and it's done her good already! Look at her, she's got quite a colour.

LIA: Oh, it's so lovely up here! So very lovely!

LUCIO: So his mind's still set on it?

DEODATA: Your father's, you mean? More than ever!

LIA: Yes . . . You'll see . . . He frightens me . . . And I feel ever so sorry for him too, Lucio . . . It hurts me to see him . . .

LUCIO: But does he still suspect nothing?

LIA: About what?

LUCIO: About what's happened to him?

LIA: Oh, no! He hasn't the vaguest suspicion!

DEODATA: Not the slightest! [*There is a prolonged pause.*]

CICO [*his manner is absorbed, for like all the rest he is thinking of the terrible thing that has happened*]: And he was dead! Absolutely stone-cold dead! [*A pause.*]

DEODATA: Yes, dead.

LIA: I saw him with my own eyes . . .

LUCIO [*deliberately, meaningfully*]: Dead?

LIA: Yes.

LUCIO: Well, in that case, you must tell him! Dead. You too must tell him that he was dead.

LIA: Dead, yes, dead.

DEODATA: We all saw him!

CICO: Dead.

DEODATA: Monsignor Lelli as well!

CICO: Yes, him as well. Dead. He got a good view of him. And then there were the doctors who examined him and *said* he was dead!

DEODATA: One of them wrote the death-certificate. [*A pause.*]

LUCIO [*to* LIA]: It *was* you, *wasn't* it?

LIA: Me? What about me?

LUCIO: It was you who got them to send for Dr Gionni?

LIA: Oh, yes! It was I who . . . Yes, I did! I started to shout at them! Nobody wanted to at first!

DEODATA: I didn't want to because . . . Well, because I didn't believe it was possible!

CICO: And Monsignor Lelli didn't want to either! He certainly *didn't* want to! I was the one that ran off to fetch Dr Gionni! I wanted to see too . . . I mean, what he'd do . . . With a corpse stuck there in front of him!

LUCIO: And then?

LIA: You know, it happened immediately! Immediately!

LUCIO: What did?

LIA: His heart started beating again! And his face . . . Instead of being all white . . . As it had been . . .

CICO: White as white . . .

DEODATA: Like wax . . .

LIA: Came back to life again immediately . . . Oh, I don't know how to describe it to you! . . . You could see . . . You

could see that the life-blood was beginning to flow again
in his veins . . .

DEODATA: And the breath was stirring in his breast . . .

CICO: His lips opened again . . .

LIA: Yes! Oh, how wonderful it was! You could just see them
moving! Ever so slightly! Oh, the joy I felt then! There he
lay . . . Still not conscious of life . . . But he wasn't dead
any longer! Joy . . . But . . . At the same time . . . Something . . . Something *terrifying*!

DEODATA [*there is a sombreness in her voice; her words come
slowly, emphatically*]: It makes me tremble still, just to think
of it. [*A long pause.*]

CICO [*softly, to* LUCIO, *as if in confidence – a diabolical note in his
voice*]: You were quite right, you know, to throw away
your cassock.

DEODATA [*instantly, to* CICO, *her voice loud and harsh*]: No!
Don't say that! You're not to say that!

CICO: It just slipped out! [*And he puts his hand over his mouth.*]

DEODATA: You promised me you wouldn't say that.

CICO: Yes, I promised you I wouldn't *say* it! But I go on
thinking it all right! With a vengeance! [*To* LUCIO] You
do realize, don't you, that . . . ? *Dead!* . . . And he doesn't
know a thing about it! Where's he been? He ought to
know . . . And he doesn't! If he doesn't even know he's
been dead, that's a sure sign that when we die, there's
nothing on the other side . . . Nothing at all. [*A pause.*]

LIA [*gives a strange little laugh – it's almost as if she were laughing
secretly to herself*]: My funny little wings, Deodata . . . *M'm?*
Those funny little angel's wings. I was to get them so as to
make up for not being able to walk down here in this world.
It's good-bye, then, to flying about in Heaven!

LUCIO [*moved*]: No, Lia . . .

LIA [*gently*]: But, if Paradise doesn't exist . . .

[*There is a pause. Then* CICO'*s voice cuts into the silence,
the words coming slowly, sombrely*]

CICO: The Lord's other house . . . The one up there . . . For all who have suffered in patient resignation down here on earth . . .

DEODATA [*her voice too is slow and sombre*]: And who abstained from pleasure that they might not fall into sin . . .

CICO [*slowly, sombrely*]: Those who are sore distrest and those who have been cast out from their inheritance . . .

DEODATA [*slowly, sombrely*]: The Good Tidings of Jesus Christ . . .

CICO [*his voice still sombre, still slow*]: Nothing . . . Nothing left at all.

[*During these last lines the faint sound of carriage bells has been heard. This sound has now stopped. There is a moment of expectancy, instinct with dismay and anguish.* DR GIONNI *comes in up Back.*]

GIONNI: Shh, everybody! Shh! Shh! He's coming. He knows.

LUCIO: He's found out?

[GIONNI *gives an affirmative nod of the head. Into the silence that falls on-stage – a silence heavy with the weight of all that dismay and anguish –* DIEGO SPINA *enters. He comes in up Back and advances down-stage, followed at some distance by* MONSIGNOR LELLI *and* MARRA, *the notary. He sees no one. He steps off the raised portion between the two pillars, comes over to the table, and falls into a seat beside it. He is white with terror, and his eyes are wide open, gazing into vacancy. Everybody looks at him in an agony of suspense and dismay, continuing to maintain that silence which is, in fact, the utterly terrified silence of life when it is brought face to face with death.*]

ACT THREE

The scene is the same as in Act Two, a few minutes later.
  [*When the curtain rises the audience sees once again the same
  tableau as that on which the preceding act concluded . . . That's
  to say, the same characters are in the same positions and caught
  in the same attitudes. Only* DIEGO SPINA *and* LUCIO *are
  missing. Shortly after the curtain goes up* LUCIO *comes down
  the stairs Right and everyone turns and looks at him anxiously.*]

LUCIO: He's locked himself in.

LIA: Did you call him?

LUCIO: I tried to get him to open the door and let me in.

MONSIGNOR LELLI: Wouldn't he?

LUCIO: No.

DEODATA: Didn't he even answer you?

LUCIO: Well, when I kept on and on calling him he shouted,
  'Go away!' [*Pause.*]

GIONNI [*apprehension in his voice*]: You go up, Monsignor!
  You go on up and have a try!

LUCIO: No, Monsignor. From the tone of his voice when he
  ordered me to go away . . . Well, I'm quite certain that at
  this moment he'd refuse to see you, too. Don't go up.
  [*Pause.*]

MONSIGNOR LELLI: It's terrible. [*Pause.*]

LUCIO: Perhaps it's all for the best that he should be alone
  while he sounds the abyss into which his faith has plunged.
  And then God will rise again in him.

MONSIGNOR LELLI [*shocked, severe*]: God? What God do you
  think is ever likely to rise again in him?

LUCIO [*simply*]: That God who dwells in all of us, Monsignor,
  and who has set us upon our feet.

MONSIGNOR LELLI [*in his pulpit-voice, but sincerely*]: Upon our feet? What do you mean, upon our feet? Can't you see? Here we are, our knees trembling with terror! And your little sister there . . . Look at her! . . . She is not on her feet. You make the earth fall away beneath us . . . Set a yawning abyss under every one of us . . . And then you say we are on our feet! Look at that woman! [*A gesture in the direction of* DEODATA.] Look at that old man! [*A gesture in the direction of* CICO.]

CICO [*trembling all over*]: You can leave me out of it, Monsignor! You can leave me out of this! To Hell with your God! [*He tears his red cap from off his head and flings it on to the ground.*] I've got my own devil inside me! I have, I tell you! And from now on nobody's going to bottle him up . . . Never again! [*He picks up his cap again and replaces it on his head.*] There! That settles that! And don't call me *old*! Old, my . . . *Foot!* [*Suddenly turning towards* DEODATA] D'you want me, Deodata? I'll marry you! [*He runs over and embraces her.*] I'll marry you! I'll marry you, Deodata!

DEODATA [*trying to free herself.* MARRA, *all the while, is splitting his sides with laughter.* LIA *is laughing too – but hers is a different kind of laughter, almost involuntary*]: Take your hands off me! Let me go, you lunatic!

CICO [*still hanging on to her frantically*]: I'm going to marry you now! Here and now! We won't bother about the law and the sacraments! We'll get married the way the dogs do! And you'll soon see that there's no sin in having your bit of fun!

MONSIGNOR LELLI [*asserting his authority –* GIONNI *meanwhile has hastened over and, with a thrust of his hand, pushed* CICO *away*]: That will be enough of that, Cico!

DEODATA [*freeing herself*]: Oh, you're a dog all right! Oh, yes! Leave me alone!

GIONNI: Let go of her!

CICO [*rounding on* GIONNI]: Who asked you to poke your nose in, anyway?

GIONNI: We're not beasts! We're *men*!

MONSIGNOR LELLI [*to* MARRA, *who's still laughing*]: And you too, Marra! Stop laughing! Don't let's all take leave of our senses!

[*While this has been going on* LUCIO *has covered his face with a hand.*]

GIONNI [*to the notary*]: Do remember that everything can be heard upstairs! And it was you ... Yes, it was you who ...

MARRA: Quite unintentionally ... Now, you must grant me that! I was absolutely ignorant of the fact that he didn't know anything about it ...

GIONNI [*to* MONSIGNOR LELLI]: And to think that I'd come dashing over to warn his son! But how on earth was I to know that ... Today of all days! ... When he was coming over here for the very first time ... Well, I imagined that it was to have a talk with him. [*A gesture in the direction of* LUCIO.] How was I to know that he'd bring the notary with him?

MARRA: Ah, you see ... Since he wanted to draw up the deed of gift relating to the farm ...

GIONNI: Clear as clear! He'd have to be told! I repeat, I thought that he was coming over to persuade his son not to break his heart by renouncing his ...

MARRA: Oh, no! No! What I meant was ... Well, he was bound to find out what had happened. He has to sign the deed of gift. And how could I ask him to sign it if, according to the Registrar, he's legally dead? I thought he knew. So I laughingly ask him, 'Oh, by the way, have you got them to rub your name out in the Register of Deaths?' No sooner have I got the words out than I see Monsignor Lelli signalling to me ... And there *he* is ... With his face as white as a sheet ... Frowning away ...

GIONNI [*to* MONSIGNOR LELLI]: But didn't you try to ... ?

MONSIGNOR LELLI: Yes, I tried ... But he [*a gesture in the direction of the notary*] without realizing ...

MARRA: What you mean is ... Without having the faintest idea ...

MONSIGNOR LELLI: Began to talk about the miracle you'd performed ...

MARRA: But I mean to say ... Well, let me put it bluntly ... All this fuss and kerfoffle! ... Oh yes, I realize what it must have been like for him ... To hear about it all of a sudden, the way he did! But, when all's said and done ... Well, if it had happened to me ... Even if it had been a question of being dead ... For ... Half an hour ... How long was it in fact? ... Three-quarters of an hour ... Why worry? If I can give myself a pinch here and now and say, 'I'm *alive*' ...

MONSIGNOR LELLI [*drawing himself up, sternly*]: So you think that that's all there is to it? *Alive?* [*Separating the syllables one from another.*] What do you mean, '*alive*'?

MARRA: Why ... *Alive!* You're not trying to deny that, *are* you? Does it matter *in what way*?

MONSIGNOR LELLI: It matters more than anything in the world!

MARRA: Well ... The doctor here knows *in what way* ... In fact we all know really.

MONSIGNOR LELLI: But we are not put into the world merely to live! No! And the other thing that we must all of us do ... *Die* ... Is the sort of thing that ... Well, you've seen for yourselves ... To know nothing about it ... To be unable to say anything about it ... Means this ... That one feels immediately that life is extinguished ... It means that one is annihilated. [*Pause.*]

DEODATA [*breaking the silence*]: Utter despair. [*Pause.*]

CICO [*breaking the silence*]: His soul, as soon as it had left his body, ought to have appeared before the Seat of Divine Justice. It didn't. So what does that mean? That there isn't any Divine Justice. There's nothing when you get to the other side. [*Pause.*] So, Monsignor, it's Good-bye, Church! Good-bye, Faith! [*Pause.*]

LIA [*breaking the silence. Her voice is light and clear and in it there almost seems to smile – so greatly does it tremble – that anguish which is prompted by a sense of desperate need*]: God must . . . Must! . . . Exist there too!

LUCIO [*as if transfigured by a sudden tremendous onset of divine emotion*]: Yes, Lia, He is there! Dear, dear little sister, He *is* there! Yes! Now I feel that He *is* there . . . That He *must* be there! *That He must be there!* Yes, Monsignor, He must be there so that He may give back their wings to those who, on earth, lacked the power to walk upon their feet! . . . He *is* there! He *is* there! . . . Now I understand, now I feel, really feel, the meaning of Christ's word, CHARITY! Because men cannot always stand upon their feet . . . Not all of them! God Himself has resolved to build His House here upon earth, so that it shall be a promise to man of the true life that lies beyond the grave. His Holy House, where the weary, the wretched, and the weak may go down upon their knees . . . Where every kind of sorrow and every kind of pride may kneel down. Yes, Monsignor, like this . . . [*He kneels.*] Just as now I kneel down before you . . . Now that I feel myself worthy once again to put on my habit in the name of the divine sacrifice of Christ and of the faith of my fellow-men!

MONSIGNOR LELLI [*stooping and laying his hands on* LUCIO's *head*]: My son, blessèd are you, for God has stepped down from your mind and once again has entered into your heart!

DEODATA [*in joyous amazement*]: He's going to put on his cassock again?

CICO [*almost ferociously*]: But what about what happened? What about *that*?

MONSIGNOR LELLI [*still stooping over* LUCIO]: What do you mean, 'what happened'?

CICO: To him . . . Him that's up there! . . . Came back to life, and doesn't know a thing about what's on the other side.

MONSIGNOR LELLI: And who told you that God allows those who return from beyond the grave to *know*? It is your duty to *believe*, not to know!

LUCIO [*getting up*]: In God there is no death!

[*He makes his way, radiant, to the stairs Right, so as to go up and put his cassock on again.* SARA, *who has remained hidden, listening to all that has just happened, opens the door Left at this moment and reveals herself. She is trembling all over with emotion. She calls out to* DR GIONNI]

SARA: Doctor ... Doctor ... [*They all turn in utter amazement.*]

GIONNI [*going over to her*]: Oh, it's you, Mrs Spina? You were in there?

SARA: Yes. Just as he wished.

GIONNI: Lucio?

SARA: Yes. So that I might give him strength. But he's found it ... He's found it in himself ... *For* himself ... He's found the strength he needed to carry out the sacrifice ...

GIONNI: That had to be made if his father was to be saved. Now perhaps ... Up there ... When he sees him dressed in his cassock again ...

SARA: Yes! Yes! I'm trembling all over ... Oh, you can see for yourself! Now he no longer has any need of me. So I can go away. Tell him that I bless him for what he's doing. No one can possibly know better than I do just what it is that he's doing. He's talked to me about life ... About how he *feels* it! How he feels it! How he would *live* it! He's renouncing it! He is going now to put on his cassock again ... Once again he will die.

GIONNI: He himself said that in God there is no death.

SARA: Yes. It's true ... In this particular sense ... Yes, you see ... It's true in this way ... There are saints even on earth.

MONSIGNOR LELLI: To rekindle in the darkness of death the divine light of Faith ... That Faith which is charity towards

all those to whom every good thing has been denied in
life.

DEODATA: He might have kept that light burning in himself,
without waiting till he saw his father lying dead . . . And
his father and all the rest of us absolutely out of our wits
with despair.

MONSIGNOR LELLI: And then you wouldn't have seen how
God recalled him unto Himself. Neither would you have
seen how he came to realize how great was his need of
Faith.

CICO [*utterly fed-up*]: Now don't say another word! Not
another word! As far as I'm concerned what you said just
now is good enough for me . . . That God can't allow those
who come back from beyond the grave to know anything
about it . . . There, you see . . . That's good enough for me.
[*And immediately, in an undertone, just as if there were really
someone else speaking from within him*] Although, all the same,
He might allow it . . . He might let us know . . . Seeing
that we've got someone here who *has* come back!

MONSIGNOR LELLI: It would be the end of life . . .

CICO: Why would it be the end of life?

MONSIGNOR LELLI: Because life is given to you on condition
that you live it out without *knowing* . . . Simply *believing*.
And woe betide the man who believes that he knows! God
alone knows everything, and man when he appears before
Him must bow his head and bend his knee.

[*At this moment the deafening report of a gun is heard. The
noise comes from upstairs, but it re-echoes and reverberates at
the back of the stage Left. Everyone is shocked into speechless-
ness. Their first reaction is to think that DIEGO SPINA has
killed himself. They all turn and look up the stairs.*]

DEODATA: Oh, God! What's happened?

CICO: He's killed himself! He's killed himself!

LIA: No! Daddy! Daddy! Hurry! Hurry!

MONSIGNOR LELLI: Lucio's up there! Can he really have . . . ?

GIONNI [*holding* CICO *back*]: No, the sound came from over there! [*He points in the direction of Back Left.*]

[*And, as a matter of fact,* ARCADIPANE *appears up-stage Left. He is in evident distress. He is lightly wounded in the scalp, and he is holding his left temple in his bloodstained hands. As soon as* SARA *catches sight of him she screams and rushes over to him, terrified. Everybody speaks at once.*]

SARA: Oh! It's you. Who did it? What have they done to you?

MONSIGNOR LELLI: Did he do it?

ARCADIPANE: He fired at me. From the window. Oh, it's nothing! It's nothing! Look ... Here ... Only a scratch!

GIONNI: Let me have a look at it! Let me look at it!

MARRA: Has he gone out of his mind? After all these years?

LIA: What happened? What happened?

DEODATA: Your father! He shot at him from the window!

CICO: He tried to kill him!

SARA [*to* GIONNI, *who is examining the wound*]: Is it very bad, Doctor? Is it?

GIONNI: No, as good luck would have it! Nothing at all! Barely scratched him!

[*But at this moment* DIEGO SPINA *comes hurtling downstairs like a madman. He is still armed with the gun and is grappling with* LUCIO, *who is trying to hold him back.* LUCIO *is dressed once more in his priest's cassock. At* DIEGO'*s appearance there is a burst of simultaneous cries of horror, terror, entreaty, protest.*]

Oh, my God! Here he is!

No! No!

Daddy! Daddy!

Merciful God!

Hold him, Lucio! Hold him!

[*Everyone is perplexed, hesitating between courage and fear, wondering whether to fling himself upon* SPINA *and disarm him, or to get out of range of his gun. Meanwhile* DIEGO

SPINA *points the gun at* ARCADIPANE, *raises it and takes aim, shouting to* LUCIO, *from whom he has managed to free himself*]

DIEGO: Leave me alone! [*And to the others*] Get out of my way! Get out of the way! First of all I'm going to kill him! Then you can arrest me!

SARA [*leaving* ARCADIPANE *and going over to him*]: Who are you going to kill? Why should you want to kill him?

LUCIO [*running forward to shield her*]: No, Mummy!
    [*And at the same moment* ARCADIPANE, *freeing himself from the restraining hands that are trying to hold him back and out of harm's way, says*]

ARCADIPANE: No! What are you doing, Sara? Let me go!
    [*But when* SARA *has uttered her challenge* CICO *has leapt forward and hurled himself on the gun which is levelled at* ARCADIPANE. *He forces the muzzle down and grabs hold of* DIEGO SPINA *round the waist.* SPINA *struggles to free himself. They all go on talking at once.*]

CICO: Now keep still! Are you out of your mind?

DIEGO: You hound! Take your hands off me! [*To* SARA] No, it's not you I want to kill! Get out of the way, you! He's the one I want to kill! Yes, *him*!

SARA: You'll have to kill me first!

MONSIGNOR LELLI: Well done, Cico! Hold him! Hold him tight!

GIONNI [*rushing over*]: For pity's sake, Mr Spina!

MARRA [*rushing over*]: You don't mean that seriously, do you? After all these years?

DEODATA: Your daughter's here! Your *daughter*!

LIA: Daddy! Oh, Daddy dear!

DIEGO [*just going on with what he was saying, turning to* SARA *and then to the others as he speaks*]: He mustn't live one moment longer! *He must not live one moment longer!* Let me go!

SARA [*confronting him*]: Yes, let him go! I am here! Let him go, Cico! I want to see what he'll do!

ARCADIPANE: Don't provoke him, Sara!

SARA: You stay where you are!

LUCIO: Mummy!

SARA [*to* LUCIO]: And you, don't stand in the way! All of you, let him talk ... To *me*! [*To* DIEGO] What is it you want to do?

DIEGO: I don't know! I don't know! I can do anything I like!

SARA: You can do nothing!

DIEGO: I can do anything I want to! *Anything!*

SARA: Because you no longer believe that God sustains and holds you up ...

CICO: We're the ones that're holding you now! Holding you *back*!

SARA: Because of this, you've become a beast and *kill*? But not even the beasts kill in this fashion.

DIEGO: I've lost all sense of reason! I see neither rhyme nor reason in anything! There's nothing I can't do! [CICO *hasn't slackened his grip upon him. Now* DIEGO *says to him, in a tremendous outburst of rage and handing him the gun at the same time*] Take the gun, and let go of me! [CICO *lets go of him, keeping hold of the gun.*] There you are ... Now I'm disarmed! Go on, arrest me! There he is, over there ... Wounded. Yes, I tried to kill him ... The moment I caught sight of him out of the window ... Standing down there ... On the ground ... On this earth that ...

SARA: He was waiting for me ... We were going away together ...

DIEGO: No ... I mean ... On the ground ... This earth ... Down on to which I've fallen, out of the cloud of falsehood up there ... The earth ... Things ... You, you've been living here with him ... Oh, but you're not going to live with him any longer, you know! Oh no, not now! Not now!

[*And once more he springs forward, intent upon seizing her, but at once he is caught and held back again, just as at the self-*

same moment ARCADIPANE *springs forward in his turn. Once again everybody is talking at the same time.*]

CICO [*on this side of the stage – he and* MONSIGNOR LELLI *and* MARRA *are grouped around* DIEGO SPINA]: Trying it on again, eh? Oh, I shan't let you go again!

MONSIGNOR LELLI: Aren't you satisfied with what you've done already?

MARRA: This is utter madness!

DIEGO: Neither I nor he shall have her! I can't bear the sight of him any longer! Neither I nor he shall have her! Yes! Yes! I'm mad!

ARCADIPANE [*who is being held back by* SARA, LUCIO, *and* DEODATA]: God help you if you so much as try to lay hands on her! Huh, so you'd like to take her back now, would you?

SARA: No! Now be quiet! Stay where you are! This is my affair! And I'm going to deal with it myself!

LUCIO: Let him say what he has to! You must show him some consideration!

DEODATA: He's not himself! No, he's not himself any longer!

DIEGO [*carrying on with what he was saying, turning to the three of them who are holding* ARCADIPANE *back*]: Yes! Why yes, let him! Let him kill me! Let him kill me! It'd be all for the best! He's got the right to! I tried to kill him! All the crimes in the world and this as well! Only... There's this, you see... You don't have to pay for what you do ... Not a thing! ... Not if you pay for everything here! Prison? The whole world's a prison, a prison there's no escaping from! And there's nothing on the other side! I *know*! [*Suddenly addressing himself to* GIONNI] Doctor, did you enjoy yourself? Was it a wonderful joke, sticking a needle into my heart, like a rabbit?

GIONNI: But it was your daughter who ... Look at her!

LIA [*in anguish*]: Daddy! Daddy dear!

DIEGO [*flinging himself down by* LIA *and embracing her as she sits there in her chair*]: Oh, my dear daughter! Dear child, why did you do it? Was it because you wanted to make me see the havoc ... The havoc I've made of your life? [*Getting up again and turning towards the* DOCTOR] But you, you who knew all the horror that I should find confronting me when I opened my eyes again, how could you possibly bring yourself to do it? Because I was dead ... As you know ... You all saw me ... Dead ... Dead ... You saw me too, Monsignor! ... Dead ... And another doctor ... Not he ... Another doctor examined me and said that I was dead ... Signed the certificate! ... And then he ... He thrust me back into life again ... Like a rabbit ... And I knew nothing at all about it ... I *know* nothing about it! I know nothing about it now, Monsignor! Bankruptcy ... If life were a business, I should be bankrupt! I can cry it aloud to the whole world ... Bankrupt! I say it and I know! If yours is a faith that is sincere, as mine was, then abandon it! Lose your faith! Lose it!

MONSIGNOR LELLI: But your son ... Look at him! ... He has regained his faith!

DEODATA: He's put his cassock back on again! Look, he's put his cassock back on again!

MONSIGNOR LELLI: Once more he dwells in the light of God!

DIEGO [*caught in surprise, to* LUCIO]: You?

LUCIO: Yes, father.

SARA: For your sake!

MONSIGNOR LELLI: For all our sakes!

DEODATA: Yes, for all our sakes, for all our sakes, for the sake of his little sister.

DIEGO: But how? Why? Now? Now that I know ... ?

CICO: No! No! You know nothing at all! God can't allow anybody that comes back from beyond the grave to know anything! So what's happened to you is no proof of anything! No proof of anything at all!

DIEGO: What do you mean, it's 'no proof of anything at all'?

I was dead, and my soul . . . My soul! . . . Where was it during all the time that I was dead?

LUCIO [*simply and gently*]: With God, father. Your soul *is* God, father. And you call it yours. It is God, don't you see? And what can you possibly know of death, if God now, by means of one of His miracles . . .

DIEGO: One of *His* miracles? . . . But it was *he* who did it! [*Pointing to* DR GIONNI.]

LUCIO: It was not he! Do you really believe that all the dead can be called back to life by anything that a doctor can do? He himself recognizes that it was a miracle!

DIEGO: Yes, a miracle of his science!

LUCIO: If our soul is God within us, what else would you call his science and a miracle achieved by means of it, if not one of His miracles, wrought when He would have it accomplished? And what can you possibly know of death if there is no death in God? And if He is now once again to be found in you, as He is still to be found in all of us here . . . Eternal, in this moment of our life which only in Him is life without end?

DIEGO: You . . . You're talking to me like this? Now? You, for whose sake I . . . ?

LUCIO: Yes. So that you may rise again from your death, father. Do you see? You had shut your eyes against life, in the belief that you were bound to see the other life that lay beyond the grave. This has been your punishment. God blinded you to that other life, and now He makes you open your eyes again to this life . . . Which is His life . . . In order that you may live it . . . And in order that you may allow other people to live it . . . Toiling and suffering and rejoicing like everyone else.

DIEGO: I? And your sister? And what about you? I tried to . . . I meant to kill . . . And all the evil that I've done . . .

LUCIO: I take it upon myself, father, and I redeem it! If now I take up the burden of all this evil that you have done, and if I feel it . . . If I feel it to be good . . . To be a blessing upon me . . . Then that is God! Do you see what I mean? That is God's doing . . . God who sees you with your own eyes . . . Who sees what you do . . . What you have done . . . And what now you must do.

DIEGO: What must I do? What must I do?

LUCIO: You must live, father. In God . . . In the works that you will perform. Arise and walk . . . Walk in the ways of life. And leave to this man, [*pointing to* ARCADIPANE] leave to this man the woman that is his. To this mother you must yield her daughter. But you mustn't just sit there waiting, Lia . . . I feel, my dear little sister . . . I feel that you mustn't wait for me to go back . . . You mustn't wait for me to make the organ sing out . . . In Lia's name . . . Filling the church with all the glory of God's Heaven! [*He turns to his mother.*] Mummy! Mummy! Call your daughter to you!

SARA [*is transfigured, as if reflecting the divine exaltation of her son. She holds out her hands to* LIA]: My daughter! My daughter!

LIA [*she rises from her chair at her mother's call, and runs over to her on her still unsteady legs*]: Mummy! Mummy!

[LUCIO *appears as if bathed in a divine light.*]

CICO: *This* is the miracle! This is the *miracle*! [*And he falls down on his knees.*] She's walking . . . She's walking . . .

[*And all the others too, dumbfounded with joy, stand there, their lips shaping the word:*]

Miracle.

*Some other Penguin Plays
are listed on the
following pages*

TENNESSEE WILLIAMS

BABY DOLL (1233)

CAT ON A HOT TIN ROOF (PL 22)

THE ROSE TATTOO and *CAMINO REAL* (PL 21)

A STREETCAR NAMED DESIRE and
THE GLASS MENAGERIE (PL 23)

THREE EUROPEAN PLAYS
1289

JEAN ANOUILH · *RING ROUND THE MOON*

UGO BETTI · *THE QUEEN AND THE REBELS*

JEAN-PAUL SARTRE · *IN CAMERA*

NOT FOR SALE IN THE U.S.A. OR CANADA

FOUR MODERN VERSE PLAYS

1253*

T. S. ELIOT · *THE FAMILY REUNION*

CHRISTOPHER FRY · *A PHOENIX TOO FREQUENT*

CHARLES WILLIAMS · *THOMAS CRANMER OF CANTERBURY*

DONAGH MACDONACH · *HAPPY AS LARRY*

FOUR ENGLISH COMEDIES

Edited by J. M. Morrell

PL 33

JONSON · *VOLPONE*

CONGREVE · *THE WAY OF THE WORLD*

GOLDSMITH · *SHE STOOPS TO CONQUER*

SHERIDAN · *THE SCHOOL FOR SCANDAL*

*NOT FOR SALE IN THE U.S.A. OR CANADA